THE SACRED HEART
OF THE WORLD

THE SACRED HEART OF THE WORLD

Restoring Mystical Devotion to Our Spiritual Life

David Richo

Now I think of myself as living solely for the Sacred Heart.
—Pope John XXIII

PAULIST PRESS
New York/Mahwah, NJ

Cover image by Chinnapong / Shutterstock.com; elements of the image furnished by NASA
Cover and book design by Lynn Else

Library of Congress Cataloging-in-Publication Data

Richo, David, 1940–
    The Sacred Heart of the world : restoring mystical devotion to our spiritual life / David Richo.
        p.   cm.
    Includes bibliographical references.
    ISBN 978-0-8091-4455-6 (alk. paper)
    1. Sacred Heart, Devotion to. 2. Spiritual life—Christianity. I. Title.
BX2157.R53 2007
248—dc22
                                                                2006101515

Published by Paulist Press
997 Macarthur Boulevard
Mahwah, New Jersey 07430

www.paulistpress.com

Printed and bound in the
United States of America

CONTENTS

♡

To the classes of 1966 and 1967
at Saint John's Seminary
and to wise and caring guides:
Father John Connelly, Father Phil King,
and Father Dan Berrigan, SJ

All of us dearly held and lovingly called
by the Heart of Jesus,
sole fulfillment of our many journeys

ACKNOWLEDGMENTS

I am thankful to my editor, Paul McMahon, who saw value and meaning in this project and helped me in refining my work on the manuscript.

My friends Dennis Rivers and Armando Quiros provided me encouragement and assistance and remain my mentors and models of heartful spirituality.

Brother Don Bisson was kind enough to read my manuscript and make insightful comments that found their way into the final version. He is also an exemplar to me of living the life one teaches about.

I am grateful to Father Jude Hill, my friend and example of the Franciscan spirit. He granted me kind hospitality at San Damiano Friary where I was able to begin the writing of this book. He and the brothers there have been graces on the path to spiritual renewal in my life, and I will always hold dear that pearl of great price.

INTRODUCTION

In a flash, at a trumpet crash,
I am all at once what Christ is, since he was what I am....
—Gerard Manley Hopkins

While writing this book I went on a pilgrimage to the woods of Mount Subasio, near Assisi, where St. Francis had lived in contemplative retreat. I lay in the cave where the saint slept and then I walked out into nature. As I stood transfixed by the natural beauty of the place, I suddenly heard a voice asking me: "Who are you?" My mind was about to come up with an answer when I stopped myself; I felt drawn, instead, simply to wait in silence. At that same moment the leaves of the trees surrounding me shimmered in the sunlight in willowy slow-motion. The whole world seemed still and yet still moving. I realized that the leaves, and all the living things I was looking at so intensely, were *opening*. That word *opening* suddenly repeated itself and I knew it at once to be the answer to the question "Who are you?"

This was a powerful religious experience for me and, when I returned to San Francisco, I shared it with my friend, a Franciscan priest. He looked at me knowingly and asked: "Do you happen to know the prayer St. Francis spoke when he went to that mountain?" I did not know it and he told me: "Lord, who am I? Lord, who are you?" This synchronicity confirmed me in my newfound trust in *continual opening* as a spiritual path. It also fit so perfectly with the theme of the openness of Jesus' heart that

I had been attempting to describe in this book. Now I see only a unity: his heart, our pilgrimage, our path, our life-purpose as humans. I also find that as I open more, I begin to see the people and events of my life as just right for learning to practice love, the central focus of devotion to the Sacred Heart. I am hoping to share this discovery in the pages that follow.

In most religious traditions, the heart of God is honored as the center of the natural world and as the center of ourselves. A spirituality of heart is thus one that cherishes three hearts as one: God's heart, our heart, and the heart of the universe. The long-cherished theme of the Sacred Heart has preserved for all of us that same meaning. We are ready today to appreciate this good news more deeply than ever. We are ready to be both comforted and challenged by it.

The Sacred Heart is God's zeal for communion with the human world. This was consummated in the incarnation of Christ and continues in the ongoing incarnation of the divine life in each of us by grace: "We are by grace what Christ is by nature." Our spiritual destiny is to show the love that is in his heart because that love is who we really are meant to be. The Sacred Heart of Jesus is the heart we had before we were born, the heart that remains in us all through life, and the heart that does not die when we do. Spirituality is letting that reality become visible in our lifetime. In fact, this is why we were given a lifetime.

A devotion to the heart of God is not only found in Christianity. The heart of Yahweh and the heart of Allah are honored in Judaism and Islam. The heart of Buddha is venerated in some Buddhist traditions. Ancient polytheistic religions referred to the hearts of gods and goddesses. In Hindu lore, the god Hanuman's heart contains the whole universe, as does the body of Krishna. The heart is a *chakra,* a center of universal love-energy. The heart is also the *axis mundi,* the still-point in the flux of becoming, which is a dancing universe.

The revelations of the Sacred Heart tell of a God who is no longer distant but who has come close, as close as our very own "within," as close as between us all, as close as around us all. Thus a devotion to the Sacred Heart is a fully and richly mystical experience. It liberates us from dualism, God out there and we down here, and gives us a unity that is abiding and that powerfully endures within time and beyond it. Meister Eckhart wrote: "There is something in the soul which is so closely akin to God that it is already one with him and does not need to become united to him." We can say that humanity's stubborn denial of this fact is the original sin. We insist on separation when oneness is built in by grace. Jesus is the model of hypostatic union, the human and the divine in one being.

Meister Eckhart says that our attachment to our individual ego is what keeps us separate and what prevents us from recovering our true identity in God. He calls this true identity of ours "the birth of Christ in us." We are baptized and called to a life of virtue in the Holy Spirit, and the Sacred Heart is what that calling looks like. God is still creating us. When we dismantle our arrogant ego, we are becoming cocreators of ourselves because our true identity is then being allowed to emerge. The indwelling of the Holy Spirit of love makes for a complete and true identity. We are ourselves when we are living the life of love. As theologian Etienne Gilson says: "When the soul has lost its likeness to God it is no longer like itself."

Where is the Sacred Heart? The answer is mystical, as Nicholas of Cusa says of the divine life: "Its center is everywhere; its circumference is nowhere." He adds: "The universe is in us in such a way...that everyone in the universe is the universe." This is why we can speak of the Sacred Heart of the world. In fact, now we know the identity of the loving intent of the universe: the Sacred Heart. When we consecrate ourselves to the Sacred Heart, we join in that intent ever to radiate love to all without exception, ever open to receiving love without limit or inhibition.

We say of someone that "He has a good heart" or "a big heart" or "a kind heart." We are not referring to the organ of the heart but are using a metaphor to describe an inner virtue that has become visible to us. Physically the heart is a pump that makes the body thrive by bringing blood in and sending it out. Poetically, likewise, the heart is love that thrives by being given and received. The Sacred Heart does not refer to the physical heart or organ of Jesus during his life in Nazareth. It refers to the heart of the risen Christ, which is not an organ but a *field* of divine energy. This field, as in gravitational or electrical fields, is both radial and magnetic, reaching out, drawing in. In other words, the Sacred Heart of Jesus is a metaphor for how God gives out and draws in love. The Sacred Heart is thus a revelation of *how* God is love; that is, both reaching out all-inclusively and yearning to receive from all of us.

The purposes of this book are threefold: to show how devotion fits into spirituality, to make the traditional devotion to the Heart of Jesus more meaningful, and to make this devotion understandable to Catholics and Protestants alike, as well as anyone open to it. I am hoping to address three questions:

- How do we form a devotional life without getting caught up in sentimentality and superstition?
- How can the devotion to the Sacred Heart of Jesus be aligned with contemporary realizations about the cosmos, religion, and spirituality?
- How can the devotion to the Sacred Heart become more appealing to Christians of all traditions?

Our first question leads us to ask: What is devotion? The Latin word *vovere* means to vow, promise, or dedicate oneself. *Devovere* is the Latin word for dedicating oneself by a vow. By the sixteenth century it had come to mean to cast a ballot as in the word *vote*. Thereafter, *devotion* came to mean pious and emotion-laden ways of relating to a personal God or a saint. The plural word *devotions* referred to practices that fostered this experience. Mature devotion is heart-connection, how spirituality becomes heartfelt personal relationship, how it enters mystical consciousness. We lose all this when we disregard devotion as an integral part of our spirituality. This is a handbook for designing a spirituality of heart with the Sacred Heart of Jesus as metaphor.

Some Catholics today are indifferent to or even repelled by devotion. Since devotion is a feature of spirituality, this is a great loss. Devotion to the Sacred Heart in particular has disappeared in many areas of Catholic worship. This can mean less personal responsiveness to the love of Jesus for us and of us for him. We will lose so much if we let this devotion go rather than rediscover it in the light of Vatican II and all we now know about religious symbolism. Now we can reclaim the riches in the devotion to the Sacred Heart with an intelligent, scriptural, and mystical faith.

The popular depiction of the Sacred Heart may appear sentimental and saccharine. But, as we look symbolically, the image of a divine open and grace-giving heart shows what our own inmost core looks like. It is a spiritual portrait of our hearts and the heart of the universe: strongly aglow with divine fire, beaming light in every direction, and at the same time opened because it is wounded. The woundedness of Christ is a self-giving, as ours can be: "Behold the heart" is to behold our own heart; it looks like this. So the familiar image of the Sacred Heart holds a mystical vision of human-divine unity that we have been looking at since childhood but may never have fully appreciated until now.

We will not be able to make our devotion more meaningful if we hold on to biases about how it looked to us in the past or how guilt-based it may have seemed. It is ironic that a symbol of generous love became focused on our need to make reparation, that a powerful divine presence became associated with a saccharine image, that a liberating message became moralistic, that a call to universal compassion became a Jesus-and-I devotion. It is time to remove the past from the Sacred Heart and restore it to the meaning it had for the mystics and can have for us today. This is the challenge: to find in what may have become tired, irrelevant, and familiar a new and thrilling possibility for spiritual growth. Our task in the church is not to go back to our beginnings in order to understand ourselves but to go to our center, where the entire gospel is, always and now, Jesus' heart.

Our second question is about how devotion fits into contemporary realizations about the cosmos, spirituality, and our evolving moral consciousness. There are at least four phases of religious consciousness in the Hebrew Bible. At first the accent was on the *hand* of God and how God acts in human history, as in the exodus from Egypt. Then prominence was given to the *voice* of God and how God instructs us about moral living as, for example, in the Ten Commandments. The emphasis then moves to the *mind* of God and what the divine plan is for humanity and the universe as expressed by the prophets and wisdom writers. Finally, we focus on the *heart* of God and what love is.

In Christianity, this love appears among us as a person, Jesus, who shows us his heart. In the history of the church, there is a gradual awakening to who Jesus is, both human and divine. He is the archetype of our own richly graced nature, human by birth and divine in our potential for love, virtue, wisdom, and the powers of healing and reconciliation in and for the world. We are human cooperators in the divine work of ongoing creation, redemption, and sanctification of the universe. As Carl Jung says: "We are not God but we are the only stable in which he can be born."

How do we cooperate in the divine plan? Devotion does not end at a shrine or image. It is only authentic when it reaches all the way into ourselves and into our lifestyle with an utterly transforming power. This is how it challenges us. We are spiritually mature when we become different from the world around us; that is, when its values are no longer ours. We are no longer motivated by greed, prestige, revenge, or ego aggrandizement but by virtues such as generosity, humility, and selfless love. Saint Paul writes to us: "Do not be conformed to this world, but be transformed by the renewing of your minds, so that you may discern what is the will of God—what is good and acceptable and perfect" (Rom 12:2). This is reminiscent of the distinction in the early church between the kingdom of Rome and the kingdom of God. The command of Christ was to abandon the greed, hate, and ignorance of the man-made city and to live—and die—for the establishment of what St. Augustine calls the City of God. Our vocation is citizenship in that city, the kingdom of God on earth. We then live by faith, hope, and love. The result is a transformation of the world, no longer divided as sacred or secular: "This [place where we are right now] is indeed the house of God and the gate of heaven" (Gen 28:17).

Our third question in this book is how can devotion to the Sacred Heart of Jesus be made appealing to all Christians and to any spiritually oriented person? A universal feature of religion is personal relationship to the transcendent, and thus devotion is an enlivening part of any religious life. Luther and Calvin denounced devotion as sentimental and superstitious because in their time, as can often be true today, people associated devotions with forcing God to grant favors: "If I say these prayers or perform this sacrifice, I will get what I want." In true devotion the bottom line is always "Thy will be done." John Wesley, founder of Methodism, stands out as a reformer who restored devotion and piety into Protestant worship. Throughout this book we will refer to many Christian and non-Christian traditions as resources in the design of our devotional practices. We are encouraged in this attitude by the Vatican II document *Nostra Aetate* (Declaration on the Relation of the Church to Non-Christian Religions): "We acknowledge, preserve, and promote the spiritual and moral goods found in other religious traditions."

In the history of Christianity, devotion to the Sacred Heart of Jesus occurred in three stages. *The first stage* was one of inklings, beginning in the Gospel according to St. John, continuing in the fourth century with the writings of the Egyptian theologian Origen, and then expanding passionately in the medieval mystics. *The second stage* came in the seventeenth century with the realizations and visions of St. Francis de Sales, St. Jane de Chantal, and St. John Eudes, and especially in the revelations to St. Margaret Mary. *The third stage* was initiated in the mystical contributions of Teilhard de Chardin and continues now in the new cosmology and in its integration into our maturing religious consciousness. Devotion to the Sacred Heart of Jesus can grow in all denominations of Christianity in direct proportion to this integration. The first stage was biblical/mystical. The second stage emphasized sin and reparation. Third stage restored the biblical/mystical dimension and liberated us from the sin-centeredness, sentimentality, and superstition that had unfortunately crept in during the seventeenth century onward.

The heart of Christianity is the Heart of Jesus, a passionate devotedness to the well-being of humanity. To be a Christian is to be possessed by that same passionate intention. Indeed, to say that God created the world is to affirm that it vibrates at a pitch identical to the nature of God, who is love. Indeed, the pitch we were meant to live at is love. Life does not ever feel quite right unless love is the best and greatest part of it. St. John says: "We know that we have passed from death to life because we love…" (1 John 3:14). Evolution moves toward more and more consciousness ("We know") and love is the culmination of that consciousness ("we have passed from death to life because we love"). This is what Jesus meant by the kingdom of love and justice, a new era of goodness and mercy, a new possibility for the survival of our planet. The mystic St. Mechtild brings us hope when she says: "To reanimate the flood of love, God has left us the Sacred Heart till the end of time."

From time immemorial we humans have searched for God, and all the while God has been seeking us. This is the striking and unique quality of the revelations of the Sacred Heart as well as of the incarnation. Our search is called the hero's journey and its goal is love. The Sacred Heart is what that love looks like. When the Sacred Heart began to appear in human history, first on the cross and then in mystical revelations, it became clear that there never was a need to search. What we were looking for was inside us waiting for us to deliver it.

The stern-bearded creator on the ceiling of the Sistine Chapel does not seem approachable or lovable. The revelation of the Sacred Heart shows, at last unequivocally, the utter accessibility of God. The Sacred Heart is the ring of flames God places on our finger after the courtship of the ages. All we have to say is yes. Indeed, the Sacred Heart is what that yes looks like.

We do not love God as one person loves another, subject to object. Since God is love, whenever we love anyone we begin to love God, and when we love everyone we love God with our whole heart. The Sacred Heart shows us how to do that: always with fire and light, sometimes with suffering, never-ceasing in love.

Since my seminary days, I have felt nurtured by devotion to the Sacred Heart. I always knew it spoke to me in a special way. It took all these years to hear what I was being asked to do. It took me fifty years of looking at pictures of the Sacred Heart before I understood what they were saying to me, asking of me, and offering to me. For instance, I never understood that this image of Jesus was saying something different from all the others

I had seen. This time, the emphasis was not on punishment but on forgiveness, not on our search for God but on God's longing for us, not on our need to expiate but on expiation already made, not on rules but on the one command to love.

I was given the grace to make a vow two years ago to make a contribution to devotion to the Sacred Heart in the world around me. This book, which I felt honored to write, seeks to contribute to this sublime desire. I have received unexpected graces while writing this book. I have come to realizations about the Sacred Heart that have amazed me, and I share them in these pages. But nothing can compare to a living devotion that I hope all my readers will find.

Now I am praying that my words—and what they may awaken in you, my readers—will open a new vision of what the Heart of Jesus is, where it is, how it is here, and how it offers such luminous hope to our modern world. I join St. Clare in saying: "I am writing to your love." May Jesus renew in each of us a passionate devotedness to the purposes of his heart.

> *Since Christ does not release us from his fate, let us hope that we will discover in our association with the sacrament of his heart what we will be and what we really are.*
> —Karl Rahner

Chapter One

THE HEART AS A UNIVERSAL SYMBOL

The Italians have a musical notation, tempo giusto, *the right tempo. It means a steady, normal beat…on the metronome. Tempo giusto is the appropriate beat of the human heart.* —Gail Godwin

There are more than one thousand instances of the word *heart* in the Bible. It usually refers to the inner self, where our souls reside. In Hebrew symbology, the Holy of Holies in the temple in Jerusalem was considered to be a heart, as was Jerusalem itself, the heart of the world. In addition to symbolizing a center, the heart in the Hebrew bible refers to one's character. The heart also signifies our understanding of God's word and our personal decision to follow it (see Jer 31:32). In Jewish tradition, the heart contains wisdom and evil too (see Jer 17:9). Thus, it is a combination of opposites; that is, an example of spiritual wholeness. A "change of heart" is a transformation of one's personality or being in the direction of goodness (Ezek 18:31).

It was only in recent centuries that the heart referred to love. To love the Lord with one's whole heart—that is, one's character and entire being—is a Jewish and Christian commandment. Babua ben Asher, a rabbi of the eighteenth century, commenting on this commandment, said that the heart was the first part of us to be created and will be the last to die, so to love with our whole heart is a promise to go on loving till our last breath. The commandment is devotion to a personal love for God, which is an unconditional love of neighbor.

In India, the heart is symbolic of the universe. This makes sense physically since the heart, like the whole universe, contracts in systole and expands in diastole. The human heart in Hindu tradition is called *Bramapura,* the abode of Brahma the creator. The heart has perennially represented centricity since it is the center of the body. The Celtic words for center and heart are similar. The word for heart is *cridhe,* related to the Indo-European word *krd,* from which comes the Latin *cor, cordis.* In the West, heart represents feeling, especially love. It is also associated with intellect and intuition and considered the core of the entire psyche. In archetypal symbolism, a center is the zone of the sacred, and the path to it is difficult. A heroic journey, our central human archetype, is the challenge required.

To the Chinese, the heart in the human body mirrors the position of the sun in relation to the universe. In this sense, the heart is a fiery energy, an equation we will encounter later in the mystics and in Teilhard de Chardin. Master Su-wen says the heart lifts itself to the principle of light and is thus the center of enlightenment. Buddhists refer to *bodhicitta,* the enlightened heart, as the longing to heal the sufferings of the world.

Taoist Lao Tzu speaks of the heart as the lord of breath and as light or spirit. Islamic mystic Ibn al Arabi speaks of the "breath of the Merciful One" that releases infinite possibilities into the world. This is the same as the Hebrew *ruach,* the Spirit/breath that brooded over the watery void in the first sentence of Genesis.

Universally in the world of symbol, the heart is also recognized as a container. In Egyptian lore, a vase represented a heart. This representation accords with the principles of alchemy in which a vessel is the container and locus of the transformation of the leaden ego into the gold of the Higher Self. The Grail myth is about the quest for a spiritual center and refuge. The Holy Grail in Western legend is an alchemical vessel or container in which personal and universal transformation take place. In the Grail stories, the human heart is a container symbolizing the Heart of Christ, whose life-blood grants nourishment to the soul. Indeed, the heart is like an inverted triangle which stands for the Grail. Shakti, the Hindu female principle of life, is symbolized by just such an inverted triangle, as are the primeval waters from which, in Hebrew and Mesopotamian lore, all life is said to have emerged. The inverted triangle is a feminine symbol. In the opposite direction, the triangle is a masculine symbol. These two directions are joined in the star of David.

There is also a symbolic connection between a containing cave and the heart. The Sanskrit word *guha* means cave and also heart. The Upanishads speak of an inner shrine within us called the cave of the heart. A cave is an incubating place, the birthplace of the light and of gods; for example, Hermes, the god of alchemy, was born in a cave. Some rituals in ancient Greece included entering a cave and, upon emerging from it, the initiates were considered reborn.

In the cosmology of Memphis, the god Ptah conceived the world in his heart and then gave birth to it by his word. The heart was understood as the center of life, will, and intellect. This is why the heart was the only internal organ left intact in a mummy. At judgment time, it was weighed by the goddess Maat against the feather of an ibis bird. If the soul weighed more than a feather because it still had attachments, the voyage to eternal life could not be embarked upon. If it was lighter than a feather, the ship of immortality was ready to set sail. An Egyptian sage alludes to this death experience and to the mystical realization of the oneness of human and divine hearts: "My heart is my God and is content with its life deeds."

In Islam, the heart (*qalb*) stands for contemplation, spiritual life, and the point of connection between spirit and matter. In Islamic mystical tradition, the heart contains seven colors visible only in an ecstatic state. *Qalb* is related to *qabil*, to receive, and thus the heart is the center of receptivity to whatever shape the divine may take; for example, a needy homeless person asking our help or an awesome phenomenon in nature. The heart is the capacity for universal receptivity.

Sufism is the mystical branch of Islam. Hazrat Inayat Khan says: "Sufism is the religion of the heart, the religion in which the most important thing is to seek God in the heart of humankind." Sufism offers three ways of seeking God. The first is to see divinity in every person and then show love by word and action. This entails a letting go of self-absorption and an ever-increasing concern for those around us. The second way is to extend our love toward those whom we do not see, a style we will see in the Buddhist practice of loving-kindness. The third way of realizing the Sufi ideal is to acknowledge and be thankful for grace and to be open to guidance from God.

In Sufi tradition, the heart is eternity, light, and divinity. It is the center of consciousness and the vehicle by which God sees us. In Sufi tradition, God breathing life into Adam means that a heart was given to him: "The heart is the center of divine consciousness and the circumference of the circle of all that is," wrote Sufi mystic Jili. In the "Ring of the Dove" by Ibn Hazm we find this mystical stanza: "Love came as a guest into my heart, / My soul then opened, so that love could dine in me."

God, speaking in the Koran, affirms this marvelous realization: "Heaven and earth cannot hold me but I am contained within the heart of my servant." The heart is the point at which a mortal being encounters God. Sufi mystics sometimes call the heart "the throne of mercy" manifesting love from God to us. God's rule is a rule of love. This means that a loving heart in any of us mirrors God to the world. To be made in the image and likeness of God means that we can be fulfilled only by a life of love. Only loving keeps us true to our human nature. This may be why the Islamic sage Yunus Emre advised: "When you seek God, seek him in your heart."

The symbol of the Sufi Order is a heart with wings. The heart is considered to be both earthly and heavenly. The heart receives the Holy Spirit, which rises to heaven, symbolized by wings. Hazrat Inayat Khan says: "Realizing that love is a divine spark in one's heart, one keeps blowing on that spark until a flame rises to illuminate the path of one's life." For the Sufis, love leads to heart-knowledge, and intuitive mystical knowledge comes through an organ of discernment called "the eye of the heart." This is an immaterial reality that sees all that is in heavenly light, the light that is the raiment of God. "I have seen the Lord with my heart's eye," says al-Hallaj.

This theme of light is echoed in the *Egyptian Book of the Dead:* "I long for nothing but to live as a light within, to enter God's heart singing a song so stirring that even slaves at the mill and asses in the field might raise their heads and answer" (translation by Normandi Ellis). Notice how the heart of God is a source of joy, and nature responds. We see this same equation throughout the history of mysticism.

In the Bible, the heart is the vital center of human life, sense, intellect, and will. For instance, thoughts arise from the heart (Jer 7:31, 1 Cor 2:9). Wicked strategies come from the heart (Jer 17:9, Mark 7:21, Luke 6:45). The heart can be opened to wisdom (Acts 16:14). The heart can focus attention and will (Luke 21:14). God knows our hearts (Jer 12:3, Luke 16:15, Rom 8:27). God writes his law on the heart (Jer 31:33). Grace comes to the heart deep within us (Rom 2:15, Heb 8:8). The Holy Spirit enters our hearts (Gal 4:6, Rom 5:5, Eph 1:17). Heart refers to the innermost secret core of ourselves (Matt 24:28, Rom 10:6), and 1 Peter 3:4 speaks of "the hidden self of the heart."

"Heart" in the New Testament also refers to the center and foundation of physical life (Acts 14:17, Jas 5:5); the seat of moral nature and spiritual life, the center stage of grief (John 14:1, Rom 9:2, 2 Cor 2:4); joy (John 16:22, Eph 5:19); the desires (Matt 5:28, 2 Pet 2:14); the affections (Luke 24:32, Acts 21:13); the perceptions (John 12:40, Eph 4:18); the thoughts (Matt 9:4, Heb 4:12); the understanding (Matt 13:15, Rom 1:21); the reasoning powers (Mark 2:6, Luke 24:38); the imagination (Luke 1:51); conscience (Acts 2:37, 1 John 3:20); the intentions (Heb 4:12, cf. 1 Pet 4:1); purpose (Acts 11:23, 2 Cor 9:7); the will (Rom 6:17, Col. 3:15); faith (Mark 11:23, Rom 10:10, Heb 3:12).

In Christian theology, the kingdom of God is within the heart. The altar in a cathedral represents the heart. This resembles the Islamic view of the human heart as God's throne and of Allah as the heart of hearts and of the whole world. The Epistle to the Ephesians says: "That Christ may dwell in your hearts through faith…" (Eph 3:17).

Carl Jung wrote: "The utterances of the heart, unlike those of the discriminating intellect, always relate to the whole. In this sense, the heart shows the meaning of things in great perspective. What the heart hears are the great things that span our whole lives, the experiences which we do nothing to arrange but which simply happen to us." Thus the heart can be configured as both personal-individual and transpersonal-collective, the heart of a person's life and of the world's life. In this sense the heart mirrors the psyche itself, which includes both our personal experience and the heritage of wisdom of the entire human collective that keeps stirring in all of us.

The rational mind is most comfortable with division. It is intent upon distinguishing and setting up oppositions. Division leads to subtraction. The heart is most at home with addition. It holds the tension of opposites with serenity because it has become comfortable with paradox. Addition leads to multiplication. Both these styles are necessary at different times. The mind zeroes in on specific differences; the heart makes room for diversity.

It is clear from our cursory look at various traditions that heartful devotion is a form of mystical spirituality. Devotion grants a vision of the spiritual world as a world of heart, an exciting place in which to be alive and a fertile place in which to become who we wholly are. Awareness of our spiritual nature turns any place we are into a sacred place. The unanimous cheer of all religions is that the center of the universe is the center of our own hearts.

We notice in our contemporary world the traditional image of the Sacred Heart of Jesus in modern art, posters, and even tatoos. There is a collective consciousness of this image that resonates in people regardless of their religious affiliation. A universal symbol like this is not only visible everywhere; it is in everyone's soul.

Symbolon in Greek also means "password." The Sacred Heart is not only a symbol. It is also a passport to participation in what it signifies. This is reality/symbol *(res et sacramentum)* that contains a power to awaken us to spiritual truth and to give us an appetite for it. Then we find that life's inner meaning is the same in the Heart of Jesus as in our heart, as in the heart of the world. The Sacred Heart of Jesus is indeed the center of the mystical body of humanity and the universe. Images of the Sacred Heart show Christ not only showing his heart but offering it, the center of his being, to us. The center and heart of divinity is given to each of us individually; that is, as part of our relationship to Jesus. Life's meaning is revealed as the giving and receiving of divine love. Devotion is then a life of gratitude.

> *The heart is a sanctuary at the center of which is a little space wherein the Great Spirit abides.*
> —Black Elk, Sioux

Chapter Two

OUR WOUNDED HEART, OUR OPENED HEART

His opened heart never ceases to blaze with love for us....
—Preface of the Mass of the Sacred Heart

Suffering and grief happen to all of us in the human family and in our own families. The betrayals, disappointments, and abandonments are wounds, the same as those of Jesus. Are our hearts wounded because we are being punished? Suffering is actually richer in meaning than this: it is the necessary ingredient for growth and redemption. In mystery-religion initiations, wisdom was gained only after enduring trials and suffering. On the heroic journey of our own lives, struggle and pain are the necessary steps toward enlightenment. It is an ancient theme that even heavenly beings endured pain and were acquainted with sorrow before they could give their gifts of redemption to humanity. Demeter's grief for the loss of her daughter Persephone, the mourning of Isis for her brother Osiris, the seven sorrows of Mary for her son all bespeak this theme in religious consciousness.

Bread is broken so it can be shared, as in the Eucharist. A heart is broken and its suffering is shared by being told or shown to others. Hopefully, our sufferings evoke compassion in others toward us. In addition, our sufferings help us become compassionate toward others, a profound opportunity for spiritual growth. This spiritual practice of giving and receiving compassion is a form of self-healing. *We can trust that we are designed for self-healing since we are destined for being wounded.* The image of the wounded Heart of Jesus, crowned with thorns, is an authentication of this possibility. His heart, cut open and yet beaming rays of redemption, also represents the wounded healer, an ancient theme in religious consciousness. All human wounds are the stigmata when we are ministering to Christ in those who suffer.

Devotion to the Heart of Jesus in the past imposed an obligation that we make reparation for his suffering for our sins. Now we can appreciate this devotion in a more expansive way: we are called to a devoted consciousness of the sufferings of all humanity. This makes devotion to the Sacred Heart of Jesus an expansion of our hearts to include all our fellow sailors on life's tempestuous sea. Serenity results from inclusive love: "For he is our peace; in his flesh he has made both groups into one and has broken down the dividing wall, that is, the hostility between us" (Eph 2:14).

We were taught in childhood to deal with our own suffering by "offering it up" to God. In that practice we were concerned with our own suffering and how to endure it. We may now expand our way of dealing with our pain by accepting it as a path to wisdom and compassion. Then we let it be transformed within our hearts so it can be released again as love. In our suffering, we are not alone, so we show a sincere concern for others who are experiencing an identical suffering to ours. Our hearts are alchemical vessels in which selfish concerns become universal caring. Devotion to the Sacred Heart is utterly without limit—like love, like redemption.

Redemption happens through the wounds of Christ. The striking image of a God who shares human suffering, a common theme in religion, changes the question "Why does God permit suffering?" Now the question is a comment, and God joins us in our suffering: "For thou art with me." Suffering has redemptive and evolutionary value. It is a given, a law of life. Spiritually aware adults have noticed that suffering is not a punishment and happiness is not a reward. Our question is not why there is suffering but how we can relieve this here-and-now suffering in ourselves and in others. *What then shall I do?*

Teilhard de Chardin speaks to this directly and consolingly:

> For our heart to yield without revolt to the hard law of creation, is there not a psychological need to find some positive value that can transfigure this painful waste in the process that shapes us and eventually make it worth accepting?....Dark and repulsive though it is, suffering has been revealed to us as a supremely active principle for the humanization and the divinization of the universe.

Heart Energy

> *There is a paradox at the heart of human unfolding: We can only love others to the degree that we are capable of loving ourselves. But, on the other hand, we are not born loving ourselves. We develop self-love by internalizing the love of all those who have loved us. As infants, we do not make our own food; neither do we make our own love.*
> —Dennis Rivers

The energy of the heart is a power for transformation. Such transformation requires "a conversion of heart." This means letting go of our self-centered ego. It is something to intend, pray for, affirm, and aspire to. It cannot be accomplished by willpower. Effort and willpower build ego. Letting go of ego is a grace that happens when we open ourselves to powers greater than our ego. We can only ask for grace, not make it happen. We still put effort into our practices but we also let things happen as they need to. We take the steps, and then "shifts" occur all by themselves. These shifts are what we mean by grace. When we balance unflagging exertion with an unconditional yes to how things turn out, we are open to shifts happening in our lives. That is openness to grace. All that is left for us is to feel and express gratitude.

William James says: "Self-surrender is...the vital turning point of religious life." That self is ego, "I" as the pivot of life. To surrender our ego is a spiritual victory because it means that we acknowledge that we have no separate self, that our self exists only in relation to God, nature, and all our fellow humans. St. Paul says of Jesus that he "emptied himself" (Phil 2:7). Jesus did not present himself as a single solitary self but as a self-in-relationship to God and to us. He showed us that our wholeness is in connectedness and that our spiritual challenge is to remember ourselves within the mystical body of humanity. Teilhard de Chardin expresses it this way: "The organization of human energy, taken as a whole, pushes us towards the ultimate formation, over and above each personal element, of a common soul of humanity."

Our heart is the soft center of our egoless self and it has one impelling desire: to open. The heart is the capacity to open. This is the force that complements our other powers. It takes us beyond our limits. It contains our ability to reach out so it is the antidote to despair. We are spiritually coded in ways we have not yet dared even to imagine. The depths of our spiritual capacity are still unplumbed. Contemplation of Jesus' Heart shows us how deep we really are, how vast our potential for love, how high our aspiration for the light.

Heart is also our capacity to be affected, to be touched, and to be wounded. A wounded heart is an opened heart. Heart-spirituality, the essence of devotion, is about giving and receiving love. There is vulnerability inherent in all loving, which may be why so many of us find it hard to let love in. Yet being truly loved is what makes our stay here on earth worthwhile. Feeling loved equips us to maintain serenity as we face what life brings, whether it be good or evil, secure or dangerous, pleasing or disturbing. Vulnerability to "the thousand natural shocks that flesh is heir to" honors our human condition. This is a healthy vulnerability. The vulnerability of a victim seeks or allows pain or abuse and thus dishonors our hearts and our bodies too.

In the ancient Stoic philosophy there is a virtue called *apatheia*. This is not apathy but equanimity. It is the serenity beyond adrenaline-based reactions to life's twists and turns and it is a direct path to transcendent knowledge of God. This equanimity is what is meant by being pure of heart. St. Clement of Alexandria says it leads to divinization *(theopoiesis)*. This mystical realization is reminiscent of the Hindu perspective in which the inner self or soul finds absolute identity with God: "I *am* Brahman." In the Christian view, oneness is not identity but rather a unity and communion with the divine.

An opened heart also means that we are open to all the happenings of life and nature. Ibn 'Arabi, Sufi mystic, writes: "My heart has opened up to every form. It is a pasture for gazelles, a cloister for Christian monks, a temple for idols, the Ka'ba of pilgrims, the tablets of the Torah, and the book of the Koran. I practice the religion of love. In whatsoever directions its caravans advance, love shall be my religion and faith." The phrase *directions of the caravans* refers to the events and givens of life. For Ibn 'Arabi the world of unseen presences becomes real when the natural world and its conditions are envisioned with heart.

An opened heart is boundless; that is, unconditional in its scope. Once we are awakened to love as the lifelong purpose of our hearts, then feeling love for all the world becomes the meaning—and greatest joy—of living. St. John Chrysostom says: "If you have found the way to your heart, you have found the way to heaven." Thus love makes life a heaven on earth. Lutheran mystic Jacob Boehme wrote:

> On the last day we will not ascend from someplace in this world but will stay here as in our fatherland. We go home into another world: this earth, a crystalline sea, where all the wonder of the world will be seen, transparently. The radiance of God will be the light within it....Heaven is the turning in of the will into the love of God. Where you find God manifesting in love, you find heaven without traveling even one foot. And now you know where hell is too.

To find our true heart is to find our dark side too. The heart is not all bliss and goodness. An opened heart reveals who we are in all its fullness. Sin is the choice to act out our dark side—what Carl Jung calls our shadow. Our work is to turn from sin; that is, to repent and make amends. Then we commit ourselves to choices that lead us to act from light. Our mistakes are motivations. Even our faults become honey in the hive of our hearts. Ralph Waldo Emerson goes so far as to say: "Divinity is behind our failures and our follies also." This fits with the continual references we see in the words of Christ to the fact that his heart is open to and loving toward sinners. The wooing of humanity by God happens when we need his love desperately, not when we believe we are entitled to it.

In Hebrew, *lev* means heart. As we saw above, the heart is thought to have two directions, toward good and toward evil, its shadow side. *Levcha* means "your heart." In the prayer "Love the Lord your God with all your heart," the word used is not *levcha* but *levavcha.* The extra syllable in the word must be there for some purpose. The meaning suggested by rabbinical teaching is that we are to love the Lord our God with both hearts or both "inclinations"; that is, the good inclination *(yetzer ha'tov)* and the bad inclination (*yetzer ha'rah*). This is a way of affirming that all of who we are can be for God.

To soften rather than harden our hearts is to become humane. How do we deepen our hearts as well as open them? We increase our capacity to love others unconditionally. This inclusiveness makes letting go of fear a spiritual practice. We cannot do this alone. It requires grace. The belief that, if we do not do things ourselves, they won't happen leads to a sense of emptiness. Grace is the gift of God that expands and extends our love and virtue beyond what our ego is capable of on its own.

Entelechy is Aristotle's word for the dynamic purpose embedded in things. It is an inner urge in nature and in the individual psyche to open their built-in potential to bloom. The entelechy of an acorn is an oak. From the human perspective, entelechy is what unconsciously organizes us. *Autopoiesis* (self-making) is the term for the tendency within every living thing to become itself. Emma Jung says it this way: "An inner wholeness presses its still unfulfilled claims upon us."

The autopoiesis of an acorn is its inclination to grow into an oak no matter how harsh the conditions. The autopoiesis of a human being is to open to love no matter how harsh the conditions. *The Sacred Heart of Jesus is the entelechy of the human capacity to love.* Fulfilled people tend to be virtuous, altruistic, and self-giving. They identify themselves by how consciously loving they are, not by their status in society. Such individuals become more and more sensitized to the suffering around them and they respond with generosity and with compassion.

Our psychological work and our spiritual practices are sacred tasks because they help us fulfill our entelechy, our divinely infused purpose to become whole. Here is a chart that may help us see how the psychological connects to the spiritual:

Our Psychological Work	Our Spiritual Practice
Growing in self-esteem	Acting with integrity and virtue
Healing/grieving our childhood losses, abuses, or disappointments	Forgiving our parents and moving on with life
Acting assertively	Standing up for the truth
Letting go of guilt and fear	Making amends and trusting God's love for us
Building healthy relationships	Living in accord with the image of the triune God in us: forming a community of loving relationships
Working on our intimate relationships and our fears of intimacy	Loving others fearlessly as Christ loved us
Showing concern for others rather than being self-centered	Practicing loving-kindness, showing compassion, and attending to the needs of others in works of mercy
Deflating our narcissistic ego	Believing in grace at work in us and asking for humility
Acknowledging our dark side and altering our behavior for the better	Befriending our shadow side and repenting for our refusals to act with love
Expanding and sharing our gifts and talents	Hearing our personal calling and and fulfilling our destiny of contributing to the good of all humanity
Accessing our unconditional love and showing it	Accessing our unconditional love and showing it as a form of devotion to the Sacred Heart of Jesus

Ten Qualities of Love

In childhood I recall a scapular of the Sacred Heart on which was the prayer: "Cease, the heart of Jesus is with me!" This was a reply we were to make to temptation. Perhaps we are ready now to rephrase that prayer and say to our own hearts and to all our spiritual opportunities: "Open, the heart of Jesus is in me!"

A heart may open in some of the following ways, each of which is a spiritual practice that presents a spiritual challenge. Each challenge constitutes a component of a spirituality of heart:

1. An opened heart wants with all its might to develop from ego-centeredness to universal love. We then fulfill our life-purpose, which is to show loving-kindness in all that we are and do.

2. An opened heart is a grateful heart. When we choose the path of devotion, many saints and guardian angels cheer and accompany us, and we thank them.

3. An opened heart no longer believes we own our virtue and love but that they have come to us as graces, gifts from a higher power than ego can conjure. This is the power that wants us to evolve and the same power by which the whole universe evolves. St. James says: "Every generous act of giving, with every perfect gift, is from above, coming down from the Father of lights, with whom there is no variation or shadow due to change" (James 1:17).

4. An opened heart is conscious of being interdependent. Devotedness of heart then becomes a commitment to work cooperatively and never to exploit others. We are not separate beings; we are inter-beings.

5. An opened heart has a sense of trust: Everything will work out in the end—and if it has not worked out, that means it is not the end yet! We trust that all that happens to us is a grace that helps us fulfill our Christ-potential and helps us make a redeeming contribution to the world around us. The givens of life

are then met with an unconditional yes since they *are* the path. Our personal story is the path to God. Since Here and Now are the two teachings, our teacher is always by our side.

6. An opened heart is one that grants hospitality to what is new and out of the ordinary. An archetypal theme in many tales is the welcoming of unexpected guests. We see this in the story of Abraham and Sara, who give hospitality to three angels unaware. We find the same theme in Greek myth as Baucis and Philomen welcome strangers who turn out to be Zeus and Hermes. In the Book of Revelation (3:20), we hear Jesus say: "Listen! I am standing at the door, knocking; if you hear my voice and open the door, I will come in to you and eat with you, and you with me." If what Jesus looks like to us is only the familiar image we have seen since childhood, we are not yet welcoming the unexpected. We can practice opening to the unexpected Jesus in every new face we meet and in every turn our story takes.

7. An opened heart is emptied of attachment, what Meister Eckhart calls "a barren desert" when he refers to the Godhead. This emptiness is a readiness or roominess to be filled by divine grace. To use an analogy, a womb, though empty, mediates life. To be empty is not to be empty of possibility but to be open to immense possibility, another word for grace.

8. An opened heart is one that cares about nature and wants to respect and protect its ecology. An opened heart sees the divine in nature and nature in the divine. Teilhard de Chardin described this mystery as "the diaphany of the divine at the heart of the universe." We have a spiritual need to go out into nature often. The old practice of pilgrimage honored this ineradicable human need.

9. An opened heart is courageous. This means never giving up on ourselves or on God. In Christian theology, despair is considered a sin against the Holy Spirit since it means giving up on grace. Since fortitude is a gift of Holy Spirit, courage is actually an antidote to despair.

10. An opened heart no longer uses retaliation as a way of responding to evil or threat. The next section describes this commitment.

The Heart's Commitment to Peace

A public Christian presence cannot be the pursuit of influence over the powers, but rather a question of what kind of community disciplines we need to produce people of peace capable of speaking truth to power….Discipline is therefore perhaps best understood as discipleship.
—William T. Cavanaugh

We can show devotion to the Heart of Jesus that presented itself so richly in the Sermon on the Mount by letting go of our inclination to retaliate against aggression and by looking for loving alternatives. We all remember voices in our past, maybe in the present too, that say: "If someone hits you, hit him back. It someone hurts you, get back at him. If someone is sarcastic toward you, be sure to have a good come-back." Today we would call this gang mentality and behavior, not spiritual practice. And yet when we grew up, we saw retribution everywhere. A superstitious belief may have developed in us that providence is spiteful too: "They will get theirs. What goes around comes around."

As we evolve spiritually, we vow to let go of retaliation as a personal style both in small and in serious ways. We begin by acknowledging our inclination or wish to retaliate. We do this without self-blame but simply as a way of being honest about ourselves. From this confession comes our plan and prayer to become free of the need to retaliate. We eliminate the plan for vengeance from our repertory of responses to others, no matter what they may have done to us.

There is hardly any motivation for the ego to find alternatives to revenge, especially since revenge feels so "sweet."
Retaliation seems to be our built-in, default setting as homo sapi-
ens. Was revenge made to be sweet so we would be sure to
engage in it? Certainly, retaliation was useful for humanity's survival because someone is less likely to hit us if he knows we are
hardwired to hit him back.

Grace from God is our main motivation to let go of the need
to hit or hurt back. At the same time, St. Thomas Aquinas says:
"Grace builds on [our] nature." Thus, there is also a psychological motivation that can support us in our response to grace. It is
our noticing that we like ourselves more when we act kindly,
when we choose not to stoop to revenge. We like ourselves more
when we come up with a creative response to injustice rather
than simply copy what others have done to us. Healthy love of
ourselves, gentle friendliness toward ourselves, is a central feature
of devotion to the Sacred Heart.

Another motivation is our tendency to trust voices we
respect: Jesus, Buddha, St. Francis, Gandhi, and so on, all of
whom spoke out against the retaliatory instinct. If they said non-
retaliation was a spiritual value, it is worth it for us to practice it
as a spiritually beneficial path.

Actually, we have an innate alternative, something built into
our very nature. When someone apologizes or shows repentance
for wronging us, we *automatically* soften. For instance, someone
cuts us off in traffic and we can be catapulted into road rage, the
reaction of the scared and then vengeful ego. But if we see the other
driver make a motion of apology, we calm down instantly and are
less likely to react harshly. Shakespeare noticed this automatic softening and praises it in his last play, *The Tempest,* the theme of which
is forgiveness as the healing alternative to revenge:

Though with their high wrongs I am struck to the quick,
Yet, with my nobler reason, against my fury

> Do I take part; the rarer action is
> In virtue than in vengeance: they being penitent,
> The sole drift of my purpose doth extend
> Not a frown further. (Act V, Scene I)

With retaliation as the ego's sole default setting and its favorite sport, the world would soon be annihilated. This shows the necessity of spiritual practices on our part for the survival of the planet! We cannot survive using only what was installed in us from caveman times. We need the teachings of saints and sages to release other energies within us. The innate softening response we see in *The Tempest* may take practice since it may have been easily overridden or dismissed by years of engaging in vengeance and being rewarded for doing so.

The spiritual virtue behind non-retaliation is *not giving up on others*. The challenge is to love people as they are and no matter what they do. This does not happen by psychological work; it takes a spiritual or religious conversion. The word *religion* comes from the Latin word *religare,* which means to "reconnect." Truly religious and spiritually oriented people look for ways to do that in their dealings with others. Revenge does the opposite; it divides in order to conquer. Love conquers by including and reconciling.

Moreover, spiritually mature people no longer see reward or punishment as God's way of operating. Beliefs in eternal damnation make it seem that God is mean and gives up on people. This is not the message of the Sermon on the Mount, a description of the Sacred Heart and of devotion to it. Many mystics understood that God is really love *always and in every way*. In the Sermon on the Mount Jesus is not only speaking to us but speaking about and from his own heart and showing us he does not retaliate either. He shows us not only what we are to be like but what God is like.

The Sermon on the Mount, in which Jesus is the new Moses, is not only a new commandment but a new promise. The fourteenth-century English mystic Juliana of Norwich described a vision that shows how our perspective can open to this as a result of devotion to the Sacred Heart: "Holy Church taught me that sinners are sometimes worthy of blame and wrath, but in my visions, I could not see this in God....God is the goodness that cannot be wrathful....I saw no vengeance in God not for short time nor for long. God shows us no more blame than he does to the angels in heaven."

To this we can add a declaration by a modern saint:

O God, remember not only the men and women of good will but also those of ill will. But do not remember only the suffering they have inflicted on us. Remember the fruits we bought thanks to this suffering: our comradeship, our loyalty, our humility, and the courage, generosity, and greatness of heart that has grown out of all this. And when they come to judgment let all the fruits we have borne become their forgiveness.

This stunning statement was found at the women's concentration camp at Ravensbruck upon its closing in 1945. It was left behind by a Jewish prisoner and it represents a sublimely mature level of spiritual consciousness.

Theologian Karl Rahner says: "The divine love of the Eternal Word has become incarnate in the human love of Christ. It has fashioned itself a place in history and cast itself for an unmistakable role in the sinful world. Thereby it has guaranteed that love, and not righteous anger, is God's first and last message to the world."

The three quotations above—from Juliana, the Ravensbruck prisoner, and Rahner—show how the heart can grasp the opportunity to love in a way that the primitive ego cannot allow itself to imagine. Retaliation is the ego's failure of imagination, a return to its favorite resort, to an imitation of what others have done rather than to the invention of a new response. It is hard to let go of the age-old drive to strike back when our ego is bruised and indignant. We attempt to rebalance things by retributive justice rather than restorative justice. In the former we punish a wrongdoer; in the latter we find a way to reconcile.

Compassion is the spiritual practice that helps us wean ourselves away from revenge. There is always a "please don't hurt me" even in someone's rage at us. To hear it and to respond is compassion in action. Without the compulsion to retaliate we can *engage with* the other's pain. Then alienation collapses into participation and leads to reconciliation. In the cooperative model, *we* work together on *our* problem. In the verdict-and-penalty model, I react to a problem as if only *one* of us created it.

It is the human community, the persons in our life-circle, who help us know the true nature of our personal existence. This is why in Christian theology we believe in a communion of saints and a mystical body of humanity. These are doctrinal pathways to a new cosmology, a spiritual world. Faith in a holy community presents alternatives to retaliation as a wonderful possibility and engaging in these alternatives as a spiritual victory.

In a spiritual practice of nonviolence, we do not seek to overcome and control others who are aggressive toward us but rather to win them over by love. The image of the Sacred Heart of Jesus does not overcome us; it disarms us. We see an inviting, receptive openness to us, no matter how cruel or ego-driven we are. All of us are touched by love like that and we respond because that is the unconditional love we have ached for all our lives. At the core of every violent person is a hunger for just such love. A commitment to non-retaliation responds to that longing as Jesus did and this is true devotion to his heart. *Devotion means alignment of our ego-actions to the purposes of the Sacred Heart.*

Devotion to the Sacred Heart of Jesus involves an engaged spirituality. Our nonviolent work and love are both personal and communal. We care for those who are suffering and we work on reforming the institutions that create suffering. The heart is on the left side of our body, so can we say we act with heart when we become more liberal in our thinking and behavior? We look closely at our country and support it in doing good, and we speak up in the face of policies that favor war, retaliation, and injustice. We affirm a planetary spirituality and do not support the move toward profit-based globalization at the cost of ecological and human exploitation. We take action against political and economic oppression. We speak truth to power at any cost. This is heartfelt love of humanity. John Dominic Crossan writes: "Jesus was building [for the poor and the rejected] a community on radically different principles from those of honor and shame, patronage and clientage."

We begin by acknowledging the shadow side of ourselves, our inclination toward greed, hate, and delusion. We ask for the grace to see our own failings and to work on them so they change into something creative. This is how we integrate rather than deny our own dark side rather than project it entirely onto others. We are also committed to being aware of the collective shadow of humanity. This is the ongoing and universal tendency of humans to go to war, inflict torture, exact severe retaliation, make weapons and chemicals that can destroy us all, exploit the poor, engage in genocide, practice slavery, undercut freedoms, become totalitarian, and show racial, religious, gender, and lifestyle discrimination through exclusionary actions and hate crimes.

Christians cannot stop all this from happening in any one generation. The list above shows the mystery of the dark side of the human collective, which seems hardwired into our gene pool. That fact does not destroy or discourage us because we have the gift of hope from the Holy Spirit. We practice the virtue of hope by not joining any movement or activity that is based on the collective shadow enterprises. We practice the virtue of hope by protesting peacefully or by sending letters to our congresspeople in the wake of injustice. We practice the virtue of peace by continually working for justice in any little or great way we can. Though the world may call us fools, it is "for Christ's sake." Jesus described himself as a good shepherd who watches the sheep carefully. We can join him in this mission by keeping close watch on the world. The Internet and the news keep us up-to-date on where there is oppression in the world. We can respond each time in some way, no matter how small. *There is a variety of Christian callings, based on our temperaments. We can take action in a countercultural way or we can be the silent leaven of love in society—or anything in between. We are not all called to protest loudly. We also serve who pray quietly.*

To say that Jesus is lord means that he is our leader and model and that his teachings are our personal principles. This means striving to make this world the kingdom of God; that is, a world in which God makes the decisions that humans make now. This means commitment to the dignity of all humans, the fair distribution of wealth, equal human rights, seeking or planning nonviolent solutions to world problems, and fervent devotedness to being stewards of earth. Do we have that power in us? Ram Dass answers: "Every ingredient needed to generate the force necessary to change the political reality of the earth is already present and exists in every individual's heart." That heart is Jesus' heart in us and that is why we do not give up.

Devotion is cosmic, so our commitment is directed toward something immense, promising, and demanding. That is like the Sacred Heart, spacious enough to include all beings and galaxies. The danger we fell into in the past was to make devotion to the Sacred Heart a Jesus-and-I relationship with the accent on how "he will be sure to save me if I receive communion on nine first

Fridays." Now we are ready to open this *I* and *me* and give way to *we* and us. We move from ego/I to all/we. Our new devotion is about how the whole world can be saved not just our individual selves.

The Sacred Heart of Jesus is a concrete image and this makes our heart-spirituality concrete. It is not narrow but limitless in concern for others and it is shown in concrete ways: food for the hungry, clothes for the naked, homes for the homeless, love for the loveless, peace for the war-torn, reconciliation for both the victims and perpetrators of retaliation. These are the gifts we bring to the table of humanity. Indeed, gift-giving is the theme of every moment of Christ's life. He gave us his teaching, his example, and his promise to stay with us always. He gave us himself in the Eucharist on Holy Thursday. He gave us his heart on the cross. He gave us victory over death on Easter. We give thanks to him when we imitate his giving to others. Jesus lost out to the forces of death and darkness and that is the Christian path to life and resurrection.

The belief that violence works is the religion of so many of us today. We believe that violence is redemption, that which frees us and keeps us safe. To live a Christian life is to contest that. Jesus came to stand in opposition to the structures of power, injustice, oppression, and domination that make our world the dungeon it has in so many ways become. Violent revolution changes the rules but not the values so it does not work to bring about essential change. What works, according to Jesus, is nonviolent resistance to evil. How can this be done? What is the spiritual practice that can make us a force of peace?

The goal is not to submit to violence or to be a doormat but to stand firm and face it with love. We do not put up with aggression or abuse, as Gandhi says: "The first principle of nonviolent action is that of non-cooperation with everything humiliating." The second principle is to resist evil and oppression with all our might but never with violence. This resistance without retaliation means we are no longer controlled by violence. We are converted from the religion of the world so burdened with superstition that only violence works and so burdened with dread that love will make us perish.

The Sacred Heart of Jesus represents and calls forth the possibility of loving all people fearlessly. It is a universal vocation to loving-kindness. We can love those who hate us because Jesus does and because his heart is in us. This is what is meant by "Love your enemies." This gives us a greater task than that of opposing violence and speaking truth to the war-making powers. We are here to love them and, by that love and our witness, to *convert* them to the love in the Sacred Heart. Revelation 15:4 says: "All nations shall come and worship." As we said above, devotion is not personal but cosmic. We are not here to find our own path to heaven but to bring all humanity, including and especially our leaders, to heaven with us too. How do we do this? We take in and hold the tension of life-crushing fear and death-dealing aggression, instead of giving it back in kind. We hold death as Mary held the dead body of Christ at the foot of the cross, long enough that it may rise into a new way of living. Our hearts become alchemical vessels in which the dark lead of bullets becomes the gold of wedding bands. We take in and take away violence and give it back as redemptive suffering. This is the meaning of our call to co-redemption. We join Jesus, who lost out to the forces of death and darkness and thereby opened the path to life and resurrection.

Jesus saves us by taking our human violence into his heart and giving back grace and redemption. His not retaliating means retaliation has been abolished as a valid human choice. We do that now for others. When aggression comes to us, we turn away from it. If that is impossible, we hold it and diffuse it by not retaliating against it. We take in hate and give back love, take in execution

and give back forgiveness, take in persecution and give back blessing. This is how we return good for evil and this makes us disciples of the Sacred Heart. Humble of heart, we do this meekly, not
as one-upmanship or as our more advanced spirituality. We are
giving what has come through us, not from us.

In the gospel, the Heart of Jesus was touched when he
noticed that the people were like sheep without a shepherd. Our
hearts are touched when we behold sad events and injustices on
the news or in our own circle of friends. We can take their pain
into our hearts and pray that reconciliation and healing come to
all those who suffer. We are co-redeemers in this practice. This is
how we courageously join the Lamb of God who takes away the
sins of the world.

Our predisposition to fight/flee/freeze can be refined by a
spiritual commitment to the alternative of standing in love with
arms outstretched. St. Stephen, the first martyr, died with forgiveness and non-retaliation in his heart. His last words, as he was
being cruelly stoned to death by his enemies, were: "Do not hold
this sin against them" (Acts 7:60). We also read that "he gazed into
heaven and saw the glory of God" (Acts 7:55). This can mean that
he had found the strength to forgive and be nonviolent by tran-
scending his own limited ego and entering Christ-consciousness.
He did not look into his ego for courage but into his larger Self—
Christ within. We all have that identity beyond our ego name: our
real "names are written in heaven" (Luke 10:20).

By martyrdom the saints collaborated in the redemptive work
of Christ. To redeem the world is to free it from enslavement to its
dark values and from the death of the soul those values cause. The
cross does not mean that God demands a death but that God
passes through death to show that it is not the end. Jesus gives us
the grace to join in his redemptive work. Pope John Paul II
preached to pilgrims in St. Peter's Square: "Devotion to the Sacred
Heart deals with matters of the heart which call us to a deeper

commitment to Christ and to others. Christ's love becomes our love. His mission becomes our mission, the work of redemption."

The openness of the Sacred Heart of Christ and of all the saints has always been a yes to wounds, a yes to compassion, a yes to giving and receiving love, a yes to bringing peace no matter what the assaults or dangers, only a yes: "For the Son of God, Jesus Christ,...was not 'Yes and No'; but in him it is always 'Yes.' For in him every one of God's promises is a 'Yes'" (2 Cor 1:19–20).

> *We as Christians participate in the only major religious tradition whose founder was executed by established authority. This is the political meaning of Good Friday: It is the domination system's "No" to Jesus....Easter is God's "Yes" to Jesus and his vision, and God's "No" to the domination system....Jesus is Lord; the powers of the world are not.*
> —Marcus Borg

> *Love one another in your hearts, and if anyone sin against you, speak with him in peace and banish the venom of hatred. Let not revenge abide in your heart.*
> —Testament of the Twelve Patriarchs, 107 BC

Prayers

Our orientation is toward wholeness not perfection. We already and always are whole; the work is to act in accord with our wholeness within. As long as we associate Jesus or prayer with perfection, we will feel embarrassed about bringing ourselves and our lives to him just as they are. For instance, how often do we pray about our sexuality or the fun things we may do? Our prayer life becomes formal and inhibited if we can only mention what seems "appropriate and right." Jesus then becomes a statue, not a friend.

Consider speaking freely to Jesus with a wholeness of heart. The prayer below is suggested for your use and as an inspiration for your own words.

_____

Jesus, you spoke to all of us from your heart at the Last Supper when you said: "I do not call you servants any longer,...but I have called you friends" (John 15:15).

Jesus, make me your friend by opening my heart. With my heart closed, I cannot walk beside you as a companion. With my heart caught up in worldly values, I cannot follow you as my divine guide. With my heart hardened against anyone at all, I am no longer loving toward you.

Show me many ways to open, every day, every moment. Don't wait for me; open me now.

I know your heart is open with compassion for humanity. Let mine open that way too. Your open heart is inclusive. Your openness is a radical acceptance of differences. May I accept everyone as he or she is rather than being critical, blaming, or unkind.

Jesus, I am open now and here to every mysterious way you reach out to me.

Let your love take effect in my heart: deepen my love.

May my heart's desire become the same as your Heart's desire: let my heart resemble yours in all I do.

Let my participation in the Eucharist take effect by opening my heart to the cries of the world: transubstantiate me.

This means that I give up all the biases of my childhood and include everyone in the infinite circle of love you drew with your heart.

I feel your heart aching to beam its love through me.

Don't let my own self-centeredness prevent your love from reaching the farthest corners of my world and every person in it, through my every thought, word, and action.

And at the same time, may I be able to honor myself, to be who I am in the world, and to express that God-given power without fear.

Jesus, I know your heart opened on the cross. May mine open when I have a cross to bear. Like you, I know that to love is to suffer sometimes. You took on all human suffering and gave it back as redemption. Let me be fearless enough to do the same.

Your heart is the heart of the universe, on earth as it is in heaven. I do not see the world until I see your heart through it, with it, and in it. Help me hold the vision of a world of heart. Let me incarnate that vision and then celebrate that vision by being a person of heart.

Jesus, you still want the world to look like your heart. Your heart, Jesus, is an opening for social change. May I join you in that work. May that happen in and through me in any way possible.

You never give up, even when I do. I trust that you have not stopped creating me, redeeming me, sanctifying me. May I join in that work by my devotedness to your heart.

Show me many ways to open, every day, every moment. Don't wait for me; open me now. Show me what space has opened and how it can keep opening.

I have not yet found my heart until it is like yours. I point to my heart right now and say "Here you are, most Sacred Heart of Jesus. Stay through me, with me, in me." May your Sacred Heart exhilarate my capacity to love.

May all beings meet in your heart.

The terrifying immensity of the heavens is an external reflection of our own immensity....In the sublime inner astronomy of the heart...we see the Milky Way in our souls.
                                        —Leon Bloy

Chapter Three

THE HEART IN SPIRITUALITY AND RELIGION

To make the human sojourn a little less sad....
—Pope John XXIII
regarding the true purpose of religion

Our Unique Path

There are some unusual atheists. They did not believe in the existence of God but feel this not so much as a denial as a sense of loss. Their atheism is more about feeling than thought. They feel that God is the equivalent of an absent lover whom they continually miss. We recall the phrase of atheist Jean-Paul Sartre about feeling "a God-shaped hole which only God can fill."

Religion begins where this touching grief begins, with a longing—ancient in the human heart—for an accompanying presence. The central desire in all mammals, the central need for survival, is connection, being-with-others. We thrive only by a series of reliable nurturing attachments, which begin in infancy and continue throughout life. For some, this sense of belonging and of personal relationship happens also in a church community. Others locate it instead, or as well, in nature, in a family, in a support system, or among friends.

There is an accent in present-day Christian spirituality on personal transformation, interpersonal concern, and transpersonal consciousness, but not so much on a personal relationship to Jesus. Devotion is a direct path to that relationship. The form of our personal connection will differ. God or Christ can resemble someone we know. He can seem like someone we talk to and see before us or beside us. The divine can also be felt as a spirit within and around us. The forms are as diverse as we are, but relationship has one thing in common for all of us: an accompanying, reliable, available, and responsive presence. A personal relationship with Jesus happens when we go beyond metaphor and feel his presence as personal connectedness with him and with all beings.

The path of devotion involves a personal relationship with a God or master in many religious traditions, not only Christian. For instance, Dogen Zenji, a thirteenth-century Buddhist teacher, wrote: "Buddha mind...arises only through deep spiritual communion between sentient beings and the Buddha." The Pure Land tradition of Buddhism advocates expressing this communion with or devotion to Amida Buddha using similar devotional sense objects as are found in Christianity: candles, incense, prayer, images, music, and so on.

Not only is our individual sense of a personal relationship with the divine unique to us, but each of us responds to spirituality and its practices in a different way. Some of us are born with an orientation to love images; others to words; others to music, movement, art, silence, or ritual. We feel something to be real when it reaches us along the innate channel through which we are best geared to receive it. This may explain why personal symbols and personal revelations, such as those experienced by mystics, are equal in value to the symbols and revelations of a collective church.

We do best with attention both to individual *and* collective resources. When they contradict each other, we pay closer attention and honor our interior knowing, as St. Augustine advises. Interiority is soul. In fact, St. Augustine described the heart as the center of our interiority: "Whose heart is seen into? Who shall comprehend what one is focusing on, what one is capable of, inwardly purposing, wishing?" In his Platonic philosophical view, our heart is a divine abode. In fact, Plato said: "The soul is most like the divine."

Some Christian mystics experienced relationship with Jesus as an exchange of hearts. Jesus took their hearts as his own and gave his to them. The exchange of hearts shows clearly that religious practices can be tailored to individuals. This fits with the central archetype in all of us, that of a heroic journey that each of us has to take in our own way. Each of us is called to follow our own path with access to the ancient collective riches but also with our own assisting and afflicting forces, our own rituals of initiation, and our own experiences and impulses of grace. In this way of relating to religion, it is not that someone tells us how to live but that we are each called by name; that is, in our uniqueness, to act uniquely. Then we begin to see God in *this* pain, in *this* joy, in *this* political event, in *this* person standing before us. The call is now individual as we hear Martha say to Mary: "The Teacher is here and is calling for you" (John 11:28).

Some religious approaches may not yet be open to the diverse styles in which the divine manifests in our hearts. A fundamentalist view may still insist that the Bible-shaped God is adequate for everyone. But the God-shaped hole in the psyche is uniquely fashioned to fit the shape of each person's heart and mind. If the means of grace were meant to be the same, *we* would be the same, not the individuals that we so wonderfully are.

Indeed, the human psyche by its diversity is a medium for the sacred, so it is itself a sacramental reality.

> *When we get off the planet, as the astronauts and cosmo-nauts did, we can see that there are no boundaries mark-ing out the ranges of nations, or races, or religions.*
>
> —Beatrice Buteau

A Changing Image

A focus on the gentle Heart of Jesus was a long-needed lib-eration from a harsh father-image of God, to the embrace of a ten-der companion God. The image of God as the strict father originates in the psychological world. It is not a revealed image of God but one based on our own experience of our parents. The domineering father demands obedience and submission as the price of taking care us. That fearsome image was transferred to God in the many centuries in which fathers looked like that.

That nexus of obedience and caretaking may have evoked a subtle belief in us. Recall the question: "Why does God permit suf-fering?" We grew up believing that as long as we were obedient to our father, he would take care of us. This illusion is what makes us wonder why the innocent suffer since they were obedient and loyal. In reality, God only promises to *be with us in suffering* and to *help us go on loving* after *we suffer.* God does not cancel the givens of life, only helps us live through them. They then become gifts and graces. Providence is a guarantee that in the face of suffering, cruelty, death, and injustice we can go on loving. The capacity for love is God in us since God is love. This is what we mean by say-ing that it all works out for the best: not that external situations necessarily rectify themselves but that our powers of love remain intact. Faith is a grace-heightened trust in divine providence no matter what the appearances predict or how they afflict.

In recent times the image of God has changed for many people. A remote male God in the sky or a primitive and vindictive father God is no longer what fathers are like, and so that is no longer what God is like for many of us. Fathers show affection more easily nowadays and both parents show nurturance. This may explain why it is easier to think of God now as male *and* female. The male God makes rules so it becomes easy to know how to please him. Goddess energy is enveloped in mystery, so it is not so simple. Is this one of the reasons we have for so long been less oriented toward the feminine in religion?

Mothers are often more kindly and forgiving than fathers. That imago may explain why we turn more confidently to Mary than to God the Father when we are in trouble. In any case, mature religious consciousness does not limit its view of God to the father or to the masculine. It includes the mother energy. This is also found in devotion to the Sacred Heart since it is the heart of the universe, of mother earth. The church has preserved the motherly love in Mary but that love is also in God beyond gender, the Holy Trinity.

The Christian belief in the Trinity makes three affirmations about the nature of God: There is a Father energy that is creative, a transcendent reality from which all being emerges, a self-giving that is unfailing. Unlike the fathers who demand submission, this Father asks only alignment to his loving will, which constitutes our happiness and our peace. This Father is nurturing and protective but does not grant exemption from life's givens, only accompaniment through them: "For thou art with me."

God as Son shows how God becomes involved in our human story in a powerfully redemptive way. Indeed, the reality of God is revealed in Jesus in a way that is definitive and yet ever-emerging; as St. Augustine says: "ever ancient, ever new." The command of Christ that we love one another as he loved us means that we are called to love impartially and to become fully committed to relieving suffering. We show devotion by being responsive to the human condition of all our neighbors—now meaning not only next door, but next hemisphere.

A Holy Spirit reveals God not "out there," but always present and active here and now, showing us ways to fulfill our destiny of joining the forces of evolution toward ever-increasing love. The self-giving of the Father, who showed how much he gives through the Son, gives now through the Holy Spirit by grace. Jan Van Ruysbroeck says: "All things are loved anew by the Father and the Son in the outpouring of the Holy Spirit and this is the active meeting of the Father and the Son in which we are lovingly embraced by the Holy Spirit in eternal love." The Holy Spirit is a feminine energy, like that of Mary, granting nurturance, brooding over us in our darkness, awakening us to our daily works of light. The creation of each of us was God's repeating of his very first good news: "Let there be Light."

> I swam in the ocean of divinity until I went beyond the Trinity.—Meister Eckhart

The Mystics' God

> I found in the writings of those great medieval mystics, for whom self-surrender had been the way to self-realization,... that they had found the strength to say Yes to every demand which the needs of their neighbors had made them face, and to say Yes also to every fate life had in store for them....They found an unreserved acceptance of life, whatever it brought them personally of toil, suffering, or happiness.
> —Dag Hammarskjöld, Markings

Mysticism is direct unbrokered contact with God. A mystical consciousness has also grasped that the divine life is one with *our* life, not identical but not separate either. Thus experience of the depths of ourselves, where we are silent and free of ego, is the experience of God. This is what is meant by God as an intrapsychic reality. *Intrapsychic* does not mean conjured or created by the mind. Intrapsychic in this context refers to the interior truth of the psyche, what Huston Smith calls "the beyond within" and what Lutheran theologian Dietrich Bonhoeffer called "the beyond in our midst." The history of devotion to the Sacred Heart of Jesus happened mainly among the mystics. To be drawn to the mystical life and to live it in some way is the essence of devotion to the Sacred Heart.

Fourth-century church father and mystic St. Gregory of Nyssa distinguishes two directions we can take to God. In *ekstasis* ("stand outside") we go beyond ourselves to find God, and in *enstasis* ("stand inside") we find God within. Both paths are legitimate and have a place in the spiritual life. Indeed, these directions reflect the harmony of the transcendence and immanence of God. Within the self is an inner sanctuary, which St. Gregory calls *ousia*, essence, the ground of being where the Infinite abides.

The divine presence within our core is larger than ourselves, a combination of immanence and transcendence. This realization is not new to Christianity. The initiates of Mithras in ancient Rome felt an awareness of the presence of a god that nevertheless remained above them. A Christian example is that of St. Paul who heard God's voice above but felt the indwelling presence of Christ as immediate union. Thus, psyche—that is, the soul, or life—is rendered "heart" in Ephesians 6:6: "doing the will of God from the heart." The experience of St. Paul presents the divine as an inner or deep reality within but also as the goodness in us that continually diffuses itself in the world. Indeed, our expression of love for others is the presence of God in the world. The divine in our inner stillness becomes the divine in daily action and this combination is holiness.

The reason we can appreciate a divine presence in our human depths is that the human depths are not simply personal. Using the limited metaphor of depth, we can say that they are transpersonal and universal; that is, not under the influence of our limited ego. Depth does not mean far inside but ever-opening interiority, replete with endless possibility. The image of the Sacred Heart has depth when it points back to us and out to the world. Our spiritual depths are the same as those of all other beings and of nature. They are not limited or individual, like personalities, but infinite like outer space. These depths are what the mystics mean by God, an unlimited spaciousness in us and throughout the entire universe. Such a mystery cannot be grasped by logic or thought but only sensed and felt. Entering the mystery of God and ourselves does not take thought but awe.

Both the word *God* and words *about* God are metaphors. Words are only pointers. Metaphor in religious terms is not simply a literary device but refers to the fact that something has more meaning than can be accommodated by any literal definition. William James used the word *More* to refer to the transcendent. This *More* is a way of referring to the transcendent God. Reality includes *More* than can be grasped by the senses, *More* than can be measured, *More* than we imagine possible. The German Renaissance mystic Nicholas of Cusa calls God "a metaphor for a mystery, the center of which is everywhere, the circumference nowhere." Each of us and everything in nature is a center and there is no outer limit. Thus God is incarnate in us and limitless too, immanent and transcendent.

Whether we perceive or imagine God as a person, or as the *More Within* as well as the *More Surrounding* us, devotion makes our relationship to God personal; that is, full of human passion and lively energy. This is why devotion is an essential element in a relationship to God. Devotion brings personal responsiveness, feeling, and passion to our spirituality. Indeed, our lively energy is actually the urge of the Higher Self to come to life in individual consciousness. Devotion lets the life-force bloom.

The mystic St. Catherine of Genoa, referred to the intrapsychic *More* in this way: "Nor can I say anymore: My God and my All. Everything is mine, for all that is God's seems to be now entirely mine. I am mute and lost in God." In *The Interior Castle* Jesus communicates something similar to St. Teresa of Avila: "Seek yourself in me." The spiritually conscious scientist Peter Russell says: "'Be still and know that I am God' is knowing that the *I am* is God." This wisdom is our heritage, intuitively known by sages and saints, from ancient times. Mystical wisdom validates and values our humanity so definitely. God within means self-esteem is a spiritual certainty!

Jesus is the first mystic of Christianity. He prayed deeply and alone, spent long hours in contemplation, had visions, heard from and spoke to God directly without mediators, was filled with wisdom, acted with compassion, and enjoyed an intimate relationship with and devotion to God as one with himself. These are all qualities of mysticism.

Here are qualities that describe the breadth of the mystic experience. The first four are adapted from psychologist of religion, William James:

- The mystical experience is indescribable since it reaches more deeply into the realm of feeling than into that of intellect or words.
- There is a sense of knowing rather than believing. This knowing is incontrovertible with no need for feedback or validation from any outside source.
- A mystical experience is believed to be received as a grace. It is felt to be bestowed, not conjured at will or generated as a result of a spiritual practice.

- The experience is transient not permanent so it creates a longing for a recurrence. (Since desire is certainly a feature of devotion, we might infer that desire is consistent with spirituality as long as we are not attached to it.)
- Mystics access the divine directly, not through mediators. The usual phases are purgation, illumination, and union.
- A mystical experience often has a bodily resonance, for example, levitation, stigmata, or erotic sensations.
- In contrast to dogmas defined by a hierarchical authority, mystics base their realizations on experience. Remarkably, though there is no "central catechism" that mystics follow, mystical realizations are the same the world over.
- Mystics lose interest in debates about doctrinal formulations and theological distinctions. Certainty, answers, and definitions vanish into an at-home-ness with paradox. Mystics no longer identify themselves with a single point of view or position: "My way is not the only way." Religion is no longer about final answers but about opening the heart.
- Images of God as inherited from childhood or from dogmatic theology give way to a spaciousness no longer limited by specific configurations.
- A mystic feels fulfilled, so preferences vanish and there is nothing left to prove, gain, or fear.
- The mystical experience feels timeless, beyond time's limits. Joseph Campbell says: "True mysticism releases you from time and then returns you to it." This double direction is reminiscent of the mystical experience of the three disciples at the transfiguration on Tabor. They went beyond time and then back to it in order to help the possessed child at the foot of the mountain.
- Mystics grow in consciousness of others. They become more and more conscious of the love they are on earth to

bestow. St. Teresa spoke of her mystical ecstasy not as *arrobamiento* ("rapture") but as *abobamiento* ("joke")! She said that all that mattered instead was a commitment to "love lived now."

- Mystics realize that the sense of a self is not all there is to consciousness. In the mystical view, the Higher Self is usually not separate from ego and personality but intimately one with all the psychic processes. Some mystics do preserve the sense of God's transcendence, for example, those referring to "the Beloved." But for most, there is no I-Thou left but only God. Meister Eckhart states it this way: "In a breakthrough, I find that God and I are both the same....Love God as he is: a not-God, a not-spirit, a not-person, a not-image, a sheer, pure, limpid unity, free of all duality." In *The Ascent of Mount Carmel,* St. John of the Cross writes: "God communicates to the soul his supernatural being so that the soul appears to be God himself and has all that God himself has....All the things of God and the soul are one in participant transformation, and the soul seems to be God rather than the soul, and indeed is God by participation."

Mystical consciousness is called apophatic, which we can distinguish from the cataphatic experience of the divine:

Cataphatic refers to the clearly lighted path. It involves affectively and intellectually responding to teachings and images with the active use of reason, imagination, and memory in order to assimilate the truths of faith and to grow in love. This is the *knowing* mind of a believer. "I know that my redeemer lives and that I shall see him on the last day" (Job 19:25).

Apophatic is the dark path. It involves resting in God beyond concepts and actions, and maintaining a loving attention to the divine presence. This is the *don't-know* mind of mysticism. St. John of the Cross opens one of his poems this way: "I entered I knew not where and there I stood not knowing: nothing left to know." Similarly, Pseudo-Dionysius the Areopagite, a sixth-century Syrian monk and mystical theologian, commented that language about God is useless and that we have "to go beyond name and form, beyond being and concept, into the divine darkness...knowing by unknowing." This is what is meant by transcendent knowledge since it goes beyond the strictures and limits of logic and linearity. Transcendence is defined as being beyond the mortal world but also beyond logical concept, which may be how God is transcendent.

Mystic Jan Van Ruysbroeck, Flemish mystic and disciple of Meister Eckhart, wrote of the search for God as being "a wayless-ness and darkness in which we never find ourselves again in a creaturely way." He found out that God is "a simple nudity, an incomprehensible light." To find this light one "finds himself and feels himself to be that light, gazing at that light, by that light, in that light." In this sense, God is known only through God, Light of light. Van Ruysbroeck goes on to say:

> All our attributes as persons are swallowed up in the rich compass of an essential unity. All the divine means...and all living images which are reflected in the mirror of truth, lapse in a one-fold and ineffable way-lessness, beyond reason. Here there is naught but eternal rest in the fruitful embrace of an outpouring love. This is the dark silence in which all lovers are lost.

Waylessness means that, for once, our human task is not a heroic journey. Now the challenge is to have *no* path and *no* destination. This is reminiscent of the story of the Holy Grail in which the knights entered the forest to begin their search "where there was no path." In mystical consciousness our minds and its tools become disabled and obsolescent and we are glad that has happened.

Using only the intellect we might believe that God is simply a Supreme Being, a wholly Other above us. Mystical consciousness is what makes it possible to find God within. Now we can see that letting go of ego is a crucial requisite for mystical experience. The thinking mind and the inflated ego's belief in its omniscience both have to bow to a power beyond themselves. The mind has to stop analyzing and splitting reality into parts. Spiritual intuition can then allow for unity so that paradox—rather than polarized right/wrong, truth/fiction—becomes acceptable as a reliable path to truth. Nicholas of Cusa expresses it in this striking way: "I have learned that the place where you are found unveiled is girt round with the combination of opposites and this is actually the wall of Paradise where you abide! The door is guarded by the most proud spirit of reason, and unless he be vanquished, the way will never open." The "place" he refers to is the threshold to the spiritual world, the boundary crossing into the eternal. The combination of opposites is visible in the two natures of Christ, divine and human, a model of our own destiny.

Mystical consciousness thus requires a dissolution of ego as a willingness to go into the dark void, the formless definition-less space that lies at the base of all reality. There we lose our habitual sense of self. This is terrifying in proportion to how attached we are to a separate identity; that is, one deprived of universal expansiveness. A mystical experience renders thought irrelevant and that can feel like loss of ourselves and a consequent chaos. Mysticism is lofty, joyous, and peace-giving. But the price for this level of consciousness is facing terror, and it takes intense courage. St. John of the Cross says it this way: "Swiftly, with nothing spared, I am being completely dismantled." *Are we ready for that?*

In the depths of ourselves we always knew that the ego was not all there was to us. A hidden life abides in us. The mystics lived from that place and called it God. Just as only a few saw the risen Christ, only a few see the deeper reality of religion. Mysticism does not devalue religion but rather revalues it at a different level. Mystics have grasped the fact that religious maturity does not happen because of beliefs but because of ego-transcendence that leads us to act lovingly, wisely, and healingly in the face of life's inexorable conditions. These are Jesus' virtues and how he pronounced his unconditional *yes* to human conditions.

Finally, we might ask if mystical consciousness renders us less able to live life's daily routine. Toward the end of St. Teresa of Avila's life, when she wrote *The Interior Castle,* she did not alternate between moments of rapture and ordinary consciousness anymore. Her mystical consciousness pervaded her entire daily life. Her ordinary consciousness had become rapturous but she went on with her routine tasks with responsibility and patience. This fits with D. T. Suzuki's answer to the question "What if someone became enlightened while he was chopping wood?" Suzuki said, "He would go right on chopping."

> *"The recovery of Paradise is the discovery of the kingdom of God within....It is the recovery of man's lost likeness to God in pure, undivided simplicity."*—Thomas Merton

Is an Image Necessary?

Devotion to the Sacred Heart has always included an image. Most mystics say that images are an encumbrance. Jan Van Ruysbroeck wrote: "We are lifted above reason into a bare and imageless vision wherein lies the eternal in-drawing summons of the divine unity." What is the difference between working with an image as an aid to meditation and not invoking an image at all? In profound mystical states no images are necessary. Yet some mystical visions also occurred in connection to an image; for example, at Lourdes or to St. Margaret Mary.

While in our conscious ego state, images help us and can even be necessary. We recall St. Clement of Alexandria: "I will give you images to understand the mystery of the *Logos*." Images are gifts of revelation. The Logos refers to Christ as the incarnate Word: God made visible. St. Paul speaks of Christ himself as the "image of the invisible God" (Col 1:15). Thus, it is not a choice between image or no image. We can move from words to the Word and from images to vision where words fail and images vanish. Both image and no image have a place as do the visible and invisible. In addition, as we saw above, God speaks to each soul personally in the indwelling Holy Spirit and this continues for all time: "The Advocate, the Holy Spirit, whom the Father will send in my name, will teach you everything, and remind you of all that I have said to you" (John 14:26).

Some of us are image-oriented, some not. Thus images will be useful for some of us while others will learn and pray better in other ways. In any case, we hear varying reports from many mystics. Here are three examples:

Brother Lawrence says in *The Practice of the Presence of God:* "I know that for the right practice, the heart must be empty of all other things, because God will possess the heart alone: and as he cannot possess it alone without emptying it of all besides, so…it has to be left vacant for him."

Jami, a Muslim mystic, says: "It is necessary to use every endeavor to force these thoughts to camp outside the enclosure of your heart so that glorious Truth may cast its rays into your heart and deliver you from yourself and save you from the trouble of entertaining his rivals in your heart."

On the other hand, Apuleius, an ancient Roman devotee of Isis, uses words familiar to our Catholic tradition: "Poor though I am, I do all that a truly religious man can do: I keep the image of your divine face in my heart, and in that secret depth, I guard your divinity forevermore."

In the course of history, we notice a mystical response to one or more of these three: an image, the person of Jesus, and pure divine consciousness. St. Margaret Mary, in her mystical visions of the Sacred Heart, represents the first and second of these. She says: "He should be honored under the figure of this heart of flesh, and its image should be exposed....He promised me that wherever this image should be exposed with a view to showing it special honor, he would pour forth his blessings and graces."

Images and statues help create a context of devotion. They take us beyond ourselves into a spiritual realm. Among them, we are in heaven. This is especially true of long-standing symbols—like that of the heart—that issue from deep archetypal images of spiritual power. Among symbols and images, we are in the transpersonal soul-world beyond ego. We do not disparage images, but we are open to going beyond them to the mystical reality they present to us. Different images appeal to us in each of the stages of our life journey. An image that worked in childhood may not have meaning to an adult. To tie devotion to the Sacred Heart to its traditional depictions is to disregard the fact that the path is always personal and that new articulations become more apt for new stages of life.

When we say that God is the ground of being, the depths of ourselves, we are beholding the theophany of the Sacred Heart without a need for a painted image. The Sacred Heart does not then stand for something. It is a direct vision of who God is. The Sacred Heart is not simply a literal image but also a metaphor and compendium of the history of salvation and of our immediate entry into it. A metaphor is a comparison, a connection of similitude, even a union of identities. To say the Sacred Heart is a metaphor is not to downgrade its reality but to connect its reality to something in ourselves. The Sacred Heart of Jesus is *our* heart when we love as he did and does. It is not a distant object of veneration but a close-up of our own heart, honored because it is his in ours and ours in his.

To pray before an image is a valuable tradition. Images grow in power when we pay attention to them; that is, honor them and see them as calling us to our true destiny. Miracles associated with Lourdes, Guadalupe, Montserrat, and many other images of Mary demonstrate this truth. Indeed, a religious image is not simply a picture we look at but a means of prayer, a sacramental, something that speaks to us in a grace-giving way and that we respond to in an active way. A religious image thus has an intentional power that makes a promise to and a claim upon us. The promise is that we can enter divine consciousness and the claim is to live accordingly, to live by love. *This is the coded information in the Sacred Heart: a set of directions to our destiny.*

As we have been seeing, religious images are archetypal; that is, they express long-standing innate longings and powers of humanity. An archetypal image is sacramental in that it helps us glimpse something not seen in ourselves and in nature. Therefore, when a religion loses or scuttles its images, it is in danger of becoming externally oriented and overly activist. The mystical sense may be lost. Then, for instance, planetary consciousness becomes taking action for the survival of the ecology. The ecology of nature is no longer appreciated as a divine milieu. The soul *in* the world is no longer one with the soul *of* the world.

Every image in the religious pantheon is energy in our souls. We are love in the Sacred Heart of Jesus, purity and humility in the Virgin Mary, courage in St. George, and simplicity in the Little Flower. They are not other than us. They are who we can be and act like right now, who we indeed became by baptism. Thomas Merton says simply, and mystically: "God is not someone else."

God and the saints are not magical powers at our disposal. They are powers that point to our personal and universal destiny. They show a heaven on earth, full of glory. They make time a story of salvation, not simply a chronicle of events. They make a lifetime a passage into immortality, not simply a series of years. They show us where we belong, and why we are here, and when we will be more than any here can hold.

Mind-made or Real?

Since we are never outside our own psyches, are we *generating* religious experiences and realizations or are we *channeling* them? Once all is psyche—that is, the entire universe is one world soul—the question about the origins of our religious experiences becomes less perplexing. We see no distinction between interior and exterior. Our deepest reach within ourselves, our heart, is one with the core of the universe and all of this is the heart of God. We channel spiritual and religious insights because they are intrapsychic.

Then the sacred represents deeper, wider, richer—not wholly other—levels of the psyche that we have not yet contacted or that we do contact only in mystical awareness. Indeed, the sacred shows us what we look like in our truest and fullest reality. The Higher Self in each of us imagines itself—"revisions" itself—through the very same images we find in religion. The images portray the archetypes of our inner life, a pantheon we share with all our fellow humans. Religion preserves a treasury of realities that take the form of faith statements, such as resurrection or incarnation. Someday we shall see how they are archetypal names for potentials in the psyche that we can access by grace once we awaken from our ego-coma of dualism and division. Perhaps this can happen once we have the clarity and energy to face and fulfill our destiny of being free from encapsulation in ego, and thus being able to embrace wider evolutionary purposes, such as generous service to the world and a commitment to nonviolence, that is, reckless love.

In the fourth century, Christian theologian Origen saw the world as one vast being and the Logos as its soul: "The sun, the moon, and the other heavenly bodies are living beings." The mystical body of God is the cosmos. Material and spiritual worlds no longer constitute a valid division. Scientist David Bohm goes so far as to acknowledge a field of energies everywhere that is full of consciousness and compassionate love. This realization can help us let go of our goal of achieving more and more merit. We show love and act virtuously because that is who we are by grace right now, not because we want to gain points for heaven in the future. This is why saints referred to their motivation for virtue as simply "for the glory of God." That glory is on earth as it is in heaven, free from dualism. No dualism means that there is a radical oneness in all of life and nature. This grants priority to love of one another since there are no dichotomies, not even between differing humans. The new cosmology radicalizes love, which itself helps us let go of dualism.

In such a view, God is not a separate being. God is not a subject except in the sense that all entities have subjectivity when they act. The fact that the whole transcends its parts may be how God is transcendent. The autonomous archetypal psyche feels like an Other, so it is understandable that the divine feels like a Supreme Person far from us. At the same time, the ability of things and of all creatures to self-organize can be a way of being personal. This may be how God is personal.

God as creator can perhaps be "re-visioned" mystically as "the universe creates." The universe as subject is the equivalent of what we traditionally knew as God. "I was created by the universe" is not a new insight. In the ancient Orphic Greek rites of preparation for death, the soul is advised: "When you come to a black poplar you will be asked your name. Do not give your name as it was on earth. Say 'I am a child of the earth, the sky, and the stars.'" The Gospel says: "Rejoice that your names are written in heaven" (Luke 10:20).

To say that we have faith in a creator means we believe in a mystery not accessible to our left-brain style of thinking. Mystery helps us avoid reification or idolatry, in which spiritual realities become things. Mystery to us in the past may have been the equivalent of an inability to explain something rationally. In the new cosmology, to say that God is a loving father is to say that built into our universe or reality is an abiding fatherliness. This adds a sense of a nurturing loving direction to our appreciation of evolution. "I believe in God the Father Almighty" does not have to be taken literally as meaning that a personal father-God lives in the sky. That belief can also mean I am committed to trusting that a fatherly love is everywhere accessible in the world and that I am committed to showing it in my world. This is how faith comes to mean commitment. As St. Thomas Aquinas says: "Faith does not end up in a notion but in a reality."

The new science tells us that matter is more flow than mass, that atoms are mostly empty space but replete with energy and movement. We can apply this to our understanding of God: the ground of all being yet not a being, substantial but not separate, "really there" in the sense of everywhere but not "out there" as distant. Just as life is within, between, and around us, God is too close to be separate from us. This is not just a modern view. Mystics always understood that God was not a separate material being; that is, reified. In Pseudo-Dionysius the Areopagite, we read of the via negativa, which states that God cannot be known or spoken of literally, only analogically, what we referred to above as apophatic mystical knowledge. We know more about what God is *not* than what God *is*, and that is all we need to know. Historian of religion Huston Smith writes: "Belief is knowledge held with certainty but not with evidence." Faith does not mean that we always know with certainty but that we act as if we were certain. Love is that certainty, the Sacred Heart of the world.

Prayers

What moves in me when I look at your heart, Jesus?

Jesus, your heart is the center of my life and of my universe.

Make me conscious of the needs of the world and give me the grace to show your heart to everyone everywhere.

Expand my narrow circle of love so I can love with universal caring, as you do.

Show me how I can join you in evolving the world in love.

Jesus, I feel myself passionately alive in the heart of the universe and I feel your heart alive in me.

May my care about nature reflect the good news that heaven and earth are full of your glory.

May my compassion for the poor and the exploited become as tender as yours.

May I and all my fellow humans go for refuge to your heart, the treasury of graces from which we draw the strength to live on earth in peace.

Jesus, I am not always the best person I can be. I often act in ways that hurt others. I ask forgiveness of them and I ask forgiveness of you.

Your heart is in me so even when my heart becomes dark in its purposes or actions, you have not given up on me. Under each of my sins is a potential, a grace, I have not yet accessed:

When I am controlling and I acknowledge that as a trespass on the freedom of others and I repent, you grant me the grace to find my ability to be responsible.

When I am vengeful and I acknowledge that as a way of satisfying my ego and I repent, you grant me the grace to show my sense of justice in restorative, not retributive, ways.

When I am arrogant and I acknowledge that as a trespass on the equality of all of us and I repent, you grant me the grace to grow in healthy self-esteem.

When I am prejudiced and I acknowledge that as a trespass on the value of others and I repent, you grant me the grace to find discernment in the Spirit.

When I am envious and I acknowledge that as a disregard of my own gifts and I repent, you grant me the grace to admire and honor others.

When I act out addictively and I acknowledge that as harmful to myself and others, you grant me the grace to build a stronger personal relationship to you.

When I notice that I am being unfair to others and I repent, you grant me the grace to use my creativity in more spiritual ways.

I am thankful that you give me a grace in every moment to examine my conscience, repent, change, and find the light of your heart in my darkness.

In Jesus, God turns irreversibly toward us in self-communication.

—Karl Rahner

Chapter Four

THE REVELATION OF THE SACRED HEART

His heart is like those cells the bees brim full.
—Pindar

The Sacred Heart of Jesus brings love into full focus as the purpose of human living. This love is God loving ourselves, others, and the whole universe. Love means vulnerability, so Jesus presents a heart that hurts along with ours in just the same ways that our hearts hurt: by abandonment, rejection, betrayal, and indifference. In his apparition to St. Margaret Mary he said: "Behold the heart that has loved humanity so much and has been so little loved in return." Though her visions often included fear-based moralisms, the revelations she received from the Sacred Heart do tell us how God feels about us. We learn that Jesus *feels and cares about* our response or lack of response. Our own caring about whether others love us, by Jesus' example, is therefore not a shortcoming or a sign of immaturity. It is part of loving one another and God.

The revelation of the Sacred Heart shows the scope and meaning of love. It shows that nothing matters but love. It brings tenderness into religion by presenting an image of warmth, a desire for relationship, and an abiding sense of divine assurance. The warmth of Jesus is what melts our cold, cold heart and makes us more radiant with love.

64

The old pictures of the Sacred Heart in our childhood homes presented and preserved a consciousness of how God is love and how love happens in suffering. Only now do we appreciate the depth of meaning in that image. A glowing heart is a warm heart that radiates compassionate love. A hurt heart is an open heart, the gate of heaven. In addition, the pictures of Jesus were often androgynous. This fits with the symbolic meaning of the heart as feminine and the mind as masculine. The softness and approachability of Jesus in these pictures showed themselves in the work of the artists who perhaps unconsciously knew the Sacred Heart was meant to open us to the feminine in the divine.

We can trust that the ever-present heart of God is the equivalent of perceiving a loving intent in the universe. Nature is continually gracious and non-retaliatory toward us. It follows that events and life's givens are gracious, grace-giving.

The Sacred Heart of Jesus sought us with grace as far back as the birth of the universe. We are loved that much. The following words of Jesus to St. Margaret Mary highlight a dramatic power that has always characterized the revelations of the Sacred Heart: "Behold this heart which has so loved human beings that it has spared nothing, even to exhausting and consuming itself, in order to give them proof of its love, and in return I receive from the greater number nothing but ingratitude, contempt, irreverence, sacrilege, and coldness toward the Sacrament of my love." The drama resides in the point–counterpoint of Jesus' wooing us with his love, our rejecting him, and then his loving us even more ardently. This is a powerful affirmation of the unconditionality of divine love for humanity without limits and not at all contingent upon our actions or deservingness. St. Margaret Mary's devotion to the Sacred Heart of Jesus pivoted around her belief in an unconditional love that continually beams its graces and grants a serene refuge in the midst of life's fretfulness: "In his heart I sleep without care and repose without anxiety." A deep *serenity* results from that kind of yes. John Croiset, SJ, a confidant of St. Margaret Mary, wrote: "The Sacred Heart preserves unalterable tranquility because it is in such perfect conformity with the will of God that it cannot be troubled by any event."

The revelations of the Sacred Heart to St. Margaret Mary placed an overemphasis on reparation and sin, which diverged from medieval mysticism in which the accent was on a love relationship with Christ. At the same time, the revelations to St. Margaret Mary reaffirmed, in a very striking way, a certitude that God *longs* for love from us. This is a sign of God's awareness of the depth of our capacity to love. We have enough love to respond to God's desire for it. In spiritual teachings, desire is hazardous and we are warned to beware of it. Yet now we see that divinity itself *includes* desire. This was visible also at the Last Supper: "I have eagerly desired to eat this Passover with you before I suffer" (Luke 22:15). This longing of God for man is an endlessly rich and provocative metaphor for how the Higher Self needs the ego to bring its light into the darkness, as this story illustrates: During World War II, American soldiers arrived in a small, almost bombed-out town in Germany. In the central square was a statue of Christ with his arms extended in love. His hands had been blown off in the recent attack. A soldier wrote this note and placed it under the statue, which the townspeople later carved into the pedestal: "I have no hands but yours."

The "so" in "God so loved the world..." is the Sacred Heart of Jesus. The Sacred Heart shows that the divine is in love with the human; the timeless is in love with the timely; the spiritual is in love with the material. Since love means connection, in this love, apparent opposites unite. Mystics universally noticed that God-in-love never ceases to woo humanity. The wooing is not from someone above to someone below, as if there were a distance between Christ and ourselves. As so many mystics realized, the whole courtship happens within us and that is why our response is described in their visions as an awakening to our true nature, a realization of God within. In that wondrous moment, our solitary and self-sufficient ego turns out to be simply a much-too-limited identity. We feel ourselves widen with universal compassion. Then we realize God was courting us to bring us close to his heart and to give us that heart to use for the good of the world: "I will bring him near and he shall approach me" (Jer 30:21).

In the Bhagavad-Gita, Krishna, the god of love, asks Arjuna: "Give me your heart." In the last chapter Krishna makes this declaration: "Because I love you so much I will communicate to you the words of salvation....This is my word of promise, you shall come to me because you are so dear to me....I will free you from the bondage of sin, fear no more."

In the Hebrew Bible we see how God desires us but leaves it up to us to open the door: "I am my beloved's and his desire is for me....My beloved thrust his hand into the opening, and my inmost being yearned for him. I arose to open to my beloved" (Song 7:10, 5:4) Similarly, the *Talmud* says: "God wants your heart."

We are attractive in the divine courtship not because of our accomplishments or talents. What makes us appealing is how much room there is in us for God. When St. Margaret Mary asked Jesus why he chose her to be the courier of his heart, he answered: "Because you are a vessel of nothingness." That phrase is not about worthiness but roominess.

A History of Mystical Devotion to the Sacred Heart

In all the quotations by mystics in this book, and especially in those which follow in the rest of this chapter, we notice that thrilling and ardent voices that show how devotion is an intensely personal and sensuous experience of our relationship to God.

There is a god in us who, stirring, kindles us.
—Ovid, *Fasti VI*

The heart is a common theme in the Hebrew Bible, often with mystical implications. *Hesed,* the Hebrew word for love, refers to the love that is loyalty (as a knight toward a king). Thus Isaiah 54:10 refers to love as covenant steadfastness. In Isaiah 62:4–5 God shows a love that is mostly pity. God is not described as a father until 2 Samuel 7. The love that represents personal intimacy does not appear clearly except in the Song of Songs, which is a secular love poem. It has been viewed as an allegory of the love of God for Israel, but modern scholarship has generally negated this as its original purpose.

The New Testament presents a love with intimate and personal meanings. Jesus asks for love and shows it. Origen, in the fourth century, was the first to mention the Heart of Jesus in a devotional way: "John rested in Jesus' innermost heart and in the inner meanings of his teachings." St. Augustine (d. 430) wrote similarly, saying that St. John, at that moment, received "sublime secrets from the innermost depths of Our Lord's heart." St. Paulinus of Nola (d. 431) said that thereby St. John imbibed the inspiration to write his Gospel and the Book of the Apocalypse.

Christ's side, identified with his heart, was pierced by a lance at the crucifixion, and blood and water flowed out. To the early fathers, the blood represented the Holy Eucharist and the water represented baptism. St. Ambrose (d. 397) wrote: "The water cleanses us, the blood redeems us." This was also the teaching of St. John Chrysostom (d. 407). The piercing on the cross is the central New Testament reference to the Sacred Heart. The connection with baptism and new life fits with the fact that Good

Friday happens in springtime. The opposites of death and new life combine in the spiritual mystery of the wounded redeeming heart.

Church fathers also saw the Heart of Jesus as symbolic of the side of Adam from which Eve was born. So the new Eve, the church, is born from the dying body of Christ, as the first Eve was created from the sleeping body of Adam. We notice in both configurations that a wound is at the origin of sacraments and church life. Church father St. Irenaeus of Lyons (d. 200) wrote: "Living water flows from the heart of Christ."

Ezekiel had prophesized: "By the river Chebar, the heavens were opened, and I saw visions of God" (Ezekiel 1:1). In Mark 1:10, John baptizes Jesus in the river Jordan: "He saw the heavens torn apart and the Spirit descending like a dove on [Jesus]." Water usually represents our unconscious, our inner life. Water also represents the dissolution of ego, as in myths of mermaids who lure the sailors of ego into the sea of spiritual rebirth. The waters of baptism dissolve the ego we inherited from Adam and Eve so that the birth and resurrection of Christ can happen in us. Initiations and new births, in spiritual literature, happen around or in the water. Openings lead to a vision, as in the above prophecy of Ezekiel. Mystics enter the interior world of the soul and openings happen. They then may experience a vision of Christ's heart, itself opening the panorama of divine love.

We recall the image of the Holy Spirit as a dove in the above quotation from Mark. It is interesting that in ancient Greece the dove was sacred both to Demeter, the mother goddess, and Aphrodite, goddess of passionate love. Thus the dove image combines maternal caring and passion. We see this in the Holy Spirit brooding over the deep to create the world in the first sentence of Genesis, as well as impassioning Jesus with a sense of his mission, and later, gifting the apostles with the fire of Pentecost. In Greece, the dove was used in divinations since it was honored as the herald of news from heaven. For instance, in the oracles of

Zeus, his priestesses listened to the cooing of doves to find answers and solutions to human conundrums. The Latin expression in the ancient ritual was *Spiritus est qui unificat.* This means "It is the Spirit that unites." Our mystical interconnectedness is indeed a gift of the Holy Spirit. It is the descent of the spiritual from the transpersonal world into our world, as happened to Mary at the annunciation. The result is always a new order of grace built on nature and renewing the earth.

Medieval devotion to the Sacred Heart of Jesus began around the year 1000 and was entirely mystical. The Crusades brought a devotional fascination with the sufferings of Christ to European religious consciousness. Mystical spirituality focused on the passion and on the suffering heart of Jesus.

St. Anselm (d. 1109) prayed that his own heart would be pierced with the word of God, using an archetypal metaphor: "The opening of the side of Christ reveals the riches of his love, the love of his heart for us."

St. Bernard (d. 1153) wrote: "I and Jesus have one heart." In *Vitis Mystica* he also wrote: "What riches you have stored for us in your Sacred Heart. I consecrate to your heart all my thoughts. The sentiments and desires of your heart are mine....I found this heart in the adorable Eucharist. It was there I found the heart of my Sovereign, my friend, and my brother." Notice the themes: oneness and friendly companionship, our call to consecration, and the riches of the Sacred Heart all contained in the Eucharist. When he says "I and Jesus have one heart," St. Bernard is grasping what the Jesuit poet Gerard Manley Hopkins grasped centuries later, in the opening quotation in this book: "In a flash, at a trumpet crash, I am all at once what Christ is, since he was what I am."

Richard of St. Victor (d. 1173) writes: "Nothing is kinder, nothing more gracious than the heart of Jesus." All these commentaries demonstrate the accent in medieval times on the personal love of Jesus for us and our personal love for him, the essence of devotion.

The theme of entering the Sacred Heart is expressed by St. Bernard's friend William of St. Thierry (d. 1148), who wrote that we can spiritually "enter wholly into the heart of Jesus, into the Holy of Holies." Thomas à Kempis (d. 1471), a German monk, wrote: "Enter the adorable heart, the hidden heart, the silent heart, the heart of God which opens its portals to you." We enter and it is opening for us at the same time. This is the spiritual synchronicity that characterizes mystical devotion.

Mystic and abbess Hildegarde of Bingen (d. 1179) wrote: "The heart of Jesus is the divine feminine wisdom in God. The hearts of Jesus and Mary are one heart: the heart of Sophia." She saw that feminine wisdom is the core of the divine. The Sacred Heart of Jesus is the heart of the risen God and so has no gender. Our emphasis in this book on the Heart of Jesus is not meant to displace the importance of the heart of Mary. Anything said of the Sacred Heart refers to the heart of the Mother of All the Living as well. This focus on the feminine is ancient in religious consciousness. We contact and honor feminine wisdom in devotion to the Sacred Heart.

The Belgian Cistercian mystic St. Luitgard of St. Trond (d. 1246) referred to an intimate *exchange* of hearts with Christ. He asked her what gift he could give her and she answered: "I want Your heart." Jesus replied: "I want your heart." St. Luitgard is the first known mystic to receive this grace.

The experience of German mystic Mechtild of Magdeburg (d. 1280) was described by her friend St. Gertrude (d. 1302): "He made her rest tenderly on his heart and said: 'Take my divine heart wholly.' And her soul felt how God poured himself into her with mighty force like a stream." St. Mechtild also saw Christ as her spouse, dressed in green and gold: "The color of my garments signifies that my divine works are ever green and flourishing with love." In both these quotations we notice the metaphor of sexual passion, appropriate since the subject here is the joining of lover and beloved. We also notice references to nature, appropriate since the divine is everywhere in the universe.

St. Mechtild expands on both these themes when she goes on to say:

> He shows his divine heart. It is like red gold burning in a great fire. And God takes the soul to his glowing heart as the high prince and the humble maiden embrace and are united as water and wine. Then the soul becomes as nothing and is so beside herself that she can do nothing. And he is sick with love for her as he ever was, for he neither increases nor decreases. Then the soul says: "Lord you are my comfort, my desire, my flowing spring, my sun and I am your reflection."

Indeed, St. Mechtild heard Jesus say to her: "My Sacred Heart is a treasury of all graces which I confer on you unceasingly. It is the source of all those interior consolations and of the ineffable sweetness which I lavish on my faithful friends." We notice in this statement that our calling is to receptivity to Christ's love, which is not contingent upon our merits but on our openness.

St. Mechtild also reports this vision: "One day I saw the son of God holding in his hand his own heart which appeared more brilliant than the sun and which was casting rays of light on every side….All the graces which God pours on humanity come from the plenitude of this heart." This is a sublime and touching vision of unconditional consolation. Indeed, St. Mechtild taught that the Sacred Heart was meant to become our refuge and our comfort in any suffering. The Sacred Heart is a place of peace, a refuge not outside but within us.

Similarly, Johannes Tauler (d. 1361) recommends that we take refuge in the gentle Heart of Jesus ever-open to those who give their hearts to him. We will see this theme repeated below in the devotion expressed by Dominic of Treves and St. Teresa of Avila. It is a frequent Bible theme also, as in Psalm 91:2 and in Matthew 11:28.

Referring to St. Gertrude, Jesus said to St. Mechtild: "The proximity of her heart to the wound in my side means that I have so joined her heart to mine that she is able to receive, directly and at all times, the flow of my divinity." This statement is reminiscent of our more contemporary metaphorical view of the divine as the deepest reality of our humanity. In fact, a medieval woodcut from South Germany in the Museo Civico di Pavia says: "His power is given to you. *You* are eternal life." We notice that the contemporary archetypal view of religion is commonplace in mystical revelations of medieval times. To say "*You* are eternal life" is like saying that God is the deepest reality of our being and that heaven is here and now. *What theologians are phrasing so cautiously today were bursts of free speech by mystics.*

St. Gertrude, herself a mystic, described her vision with natural and sexual metaphors: "The divine heart in which every good is hidden, opened as a paradise of joy. There all the sighs of the human Christ and all the thoughts of his Sacred Heart grew like roses, lilies, and violets, and shed their perfumes." St. Gertrude then prayed: "Open to me the treasure of your most gracious heart, where the sum of my desire is stored....Through your wounded heart, dearest Lord, pierce my heart so deeply with the dart of your love that it may no longer be attached to passing things but may be governed by the action of your Divinity alone." Here we see strongly sensuous references to the appropriateness of desire, the promise of fulfillment, and, at the same time, the teaching of impermanence as well as renewal that nature presents. All combinations of opposites form one metaphor of the exchange of hearts between God and ourselves.

St. Gertrude experienced a vision of St. John the Apostle and she questioned why he never wrote very much about the Sacred Heart. He answered that the knowledge of Jesus' heart had been reserved until her era while he was instead "called to instruct the newly-formed Church about the mysteries of the Uncreated Word." This vision shows the continuity of devotion the Sacred Heart with the earliest Christian experience. The good news was always about heart.

The historian who recorded the death of St. Gertrude wrote: "Her blessed soul took flight into heaven and retired into the sanctuary of divinity, I mean into the adorable heart of Jesus which this divine spouse, in an excess of love, had opened to her." This sense of the Sacred Heart as a refuge appears in St. Gertrude's own words: "God of my heart, may Your sufferings serve as a shelter at the hour of my death and may Your gentle heart, broken for love of me, be my eternal dwelling, since I love You alone more than all creatures in the world." The Sacred Heart of Jesus as a refuge keeps appearing in mystical revelations. It is a promise and a guarantee.

In the 1230s, St. Clare of Assisi, close friend of St. Francis, wrote letters to Blessed Agnes of Prague. In Clare's third letter she says:

> I see, too, that you are embracing, with humility, the virtue of faith, and the...incomparable treasure that lies hidden in the field of the world and in the hearts of human beings, where it is purchased by the One by whom all things were made from nothing.
> Place your mind in the mirror of eternity.
> Place your soul in the splendor of glory.
> Place your heart in the figure of the divine substance.

In her fourth letter she says: "May you exclaim: 'Draw me after you, Heavenly Spouse, we shall run in the fragrance of your perfumes! I shall run and not grow weary until you bring me into the wine cellar, until your left hand is under my head and your right arm blissfully embraces me; and you kiss me with the most blissful kiss of your mouth.'"

We notice the extravagant metaphors of human courtship and are reminded that our souls are wooed, simultaneously, by a God and a companion. St. Bernard comments on the Song of Songs and actually suggests a spiritual practice of imagining ourselves kissing Christ's feet as a sign of repentance, kissing his hands as a request for grace, and, yes, kissing his lips as an acknowledgment of union. Mystics, especially St. Teresa, had no problem with speaking of their love for God in earthy or erotic terms. *Can we retrieve that mystical daring?*

It is important to realize that mystical statements, especially those of celibate women, present sexuality as an *interior* event and often as eucharistic communion. In the *Guide for Anchoresses* written in thirteenth-century England, union with Christ is strongly connected to the Eucharist: "After the kiss of peace at Mass...go completely out of body and with burning love embrace your Beloved, who has come down from heaven to your heart's bower, and hold him fast until he has granted all you ask." The sense of a human-divine meeting in the Eucharist is felt in this statement of St. Elzear to his wife St. Delphine: "For news of me go to Jesus in the blessed sacrament because you can always find me there. It is my usual dwelling place."

Franciscan theologian St. Bonaventure (d. 1274) wrote:

Since we have reached the most sweet heart of Jesus, and it is good for us to abide in It, let us not readily turn away from It. How good, how sweet it is to dwell in Thy heart, O good Jesus! Who is there who would not desire this pearl? I would rather give all else, all

> my thoughts and all the affections of my soul in
> exchange for It, casting my whole mind into the heart
> of my good Jesus....Who is there who would not love
> this wounded heart? Who would not love, in return,
> Him Who loves so much?

In these intimate words, we see again the pledge of the Heart of
Jesus as our refuge. St. Bonaventure also asks this: "My soul, if the
voice of your beloved makes you melt into love for Him, why are
you not utterly inflamed and consumed when you enter by the
sacred wound of His side into the burning furnace of His loving
heart?"

Many medieval hymns contain mystical realizations. The
earliest hymn to the Sacred Heart, "Summi Regis Cor," is believed
to have been composed by Blessed Herman Joseph (d. 1241); it
begins: "I hail Thee kingly heart most high." A hymn by
Franciscan Jacopone da Todi (d. 1306) refers to Christ writing
the names of devout souls upon his heart. This is repeated later
in the promises of the Sacred Heart to St. Margaret Mary: "Those
who spread this devotion will have their names written in my
heart never to be effaced."

German Dominicans in the middle ages, with forty-six
monasteries and seventy convents, made a great contribution to
the devotion to the Sacred Heart. The emphasis was on mystical
devotion to the passion, seeing Christ's wounds as tokens of his
love for us. This led to a spirituality of the mystery of the Sacred
Heart.

Dominican St. Albert the Great (d. 1280) wrote: "By the
blood from his side he watered the garden of the church." Our
spiritual sustenance comes from the heart of God and is ever
surging in community.

Dominican and student of St. Thomas Aquinas, Meister
Eckhart (d. 1327) writes:

> On the cross his heart burned like a fire and furnace from which the flame burst forth on all sides. So was he inflamed on the cross by the fire of his love for the whole world....The noble birth of Christ in the soul happens in the core of the soul in which is the central silence, the peace, and the abode of the heavenly birth....Into the central silence no creature may enter, nor any idea, and there the soul neither thinks nor acts, nor entertains any idea, either of itself or of anything else.

This is a profound realization about the mystical silence from which revelations arise. In our own times, Pope Benedict XVI writes: "In silence we journey inward...leaving behind the roles which conceal our real selves. In silence we bide and abide and become aware of the abiding reality."

Dominican Johann Tauler (d. 1361) wrote a book of spiritual exercises on the passion and in it he mentions the Sacred Heart fifty times. We see again the theme of contemplative silence:

> What more could he still do for us, that he has not done? He has opened his very heart to us, as the most secret chamber wherein to lead our soul, his chosen spouse. For it is his joy to be with us in silent stillness, and in peaceful silence to rest there with us....He gives us his heart entirely, that it may be our home. He desires our hearts in return that they may be his dwelling place.

This is a reference to taking refuge but this time we see Jesus wanting refuge in us, another example of the theme of God wooing humanity.

In Eckhart's and Tauler's references to silence and oneness, we can hear the words of Ralph Waldo Emerson: "We live in a succession, in a division, in parts, in particles. Meantime, within man is the soul of the whole, the wise silence, the universal beauty, to which every part and particle is equally related, the eternal One." In the Bhagavad-Gita 12:19, Krishna says: "Dear to me is he who is balanced in praise and blame, who has silence of soul, who is happy with what he has, whose real home is beyond the material world and who is full of love." In mystic and poetic voices of all traditions, we notice the universality of spiritual wisdom.

Dominican mystic St. Catherine of Siena (d. 1380) said: "*La mia natura e' fuoco,*" which means "My very nature is fire." In 1370 she experienced an exchange of hearts with Christ. At another time, she said to Jesus: "Sweet Spotless Lamb, You were dead when Your Side was opened. Why, then, did You allow that Your heart should be thus wounded and opened by force?" He answered:

> "My desires regarding the human race were infinite and the actual time of my suffering and torture was at an end. Since my love is infinite, I could not therefore by this suffering manifest to you how much I loved you. That is why I willed to reveal to you the secret of my heart by letting you see it open, that you might well understand that my heart loved you far more than I could prove to you by a suffering that was over."

This and all these statements are awesome because they signify an openness and a gift of love that is beyond human reckoning. In St. Catherine's words we also notice the role of suffering in love.

Dominican mystic Blessed Henry Suso (d. 1366) experienced an angel removing his heart from him and placing it in the heart of Jesus with rapturous love.

Carthusian Ludolf of Saxony (d. 1378) wrote the *Life of Jesus,* one of two books read by St. Ignatius, founder of the Jesuits, in his conversion experience. Ludolf writes: "The heart of Christ was wounded for us with the wound of love for us, that through the opening of his side we might enter his heart by love and there unite our love with divine love as only one love, as glowing iron is one with fire." Here too, we learn about suffering and its relationship to love.

Juliana of Norwich (d. after 1413) reported this vision:

Then Our Lord looked into His Side and rejoiced. By this sweet look He had me gaze within his Wound. He showed me a fair, delectable place, and large enough for all mankind that shall be saved to rest in peace and in love. And therewith He had me recall His dear worthy Blood and precious Water which He let pour out for love and He showed me His blissful heart.

The theme of refuge in Jesus' heart recurs in so many mystical experiences. The wound opens the heart of Jesus and offers this possibility to us too.

St. Bernardine of Siena (d. 1444) writes of Jesus: "His side opens not to release a deluge of water but a deluge of love...the secret hidden from all eternity now manifest in his opened side...the opening of an eternal temple."

Carthusian Dominic of Treves (d. 1461) said: "In this most sweet heart of Jesus is found all virtue, the source of life, perfect consolation, the true light that enlightens every person."

An illuminated manuscript from around 1500—at the Benedictine convent of St. Walburg, in Eichstatt, Bavaria—shows a heart on a cross, a eucharistic banquet in which nuns commune with Christ in his heart and his heart as the house in which the nuns live. The convent itself also housed a carved Sacred Heart. One image shows a heart-shaped frame in which a man offers a loaf of bread to a nun, while a dove with a halo offers a chalice. All this happens outdoors in nature, where Christ presents them to one another. This image was meant to be a visual aid for meditation for nuns at the abbey. We are seeing devotion from the inside out (mystical communion and interiority), not from the outside in (ritual practices and action).

St. Teresa of Avila (d. 1582) recommended that we make the wounded heart of Jesus our secure place of refuge. Here we see the combination of the themes of refuge and of the exchange of hearts. She went on to declare: "The important thing is not to think much but to love much and to do that which stirs us to love." Upon her conversion she began a devotion to the heart of God as it can be found in others.

In her writings we also see the themes of fire and bodily sensation in mystical rapture:

> It pleased the Lord that I should see an angel...very beautiful, his face so aflame....In his hands I saw a long golden spear and at the end of the iron tip I seemed to see a point of fire. With this he seemed to pierce my heart several times so that it penetrated to my entrails. When he drew it out, I thought he was drawing them out with it and he left me completely afire with a great love for God. The pain was so sharp that it made me utter several moans; and so excessive was the sweetness caused me by this intense pain that one can never wish to lose it, nor will one's soul be content with anything less. It is not bodily pain, but spiritual, though the body has a share in it—indeed, a great share.

The Carthusian monk Lanspergius (d. 1539) suggested that Christians keep a picture of the Sacred Heart in their homes as a way of fostering devotion. He also suggested kissing the picture, which shows the power of images to make a spiritual reality present. This is perhaps the first reference to encouraging people to have and honor a picture of the Sacred Heart. It was to become a plea from Jesus through St. Margaret Mary in the seventeenth century.

French bishop Cornelius Jansenius (d. 1638) taught that the body is evil and that pleasures of all kinds were suspect or sinful. There were as many as fifty dioceses in France in the seventeenth century that were administered by Jansenist bishops. The church recommended devotion to the Sacred Heart of Jesus as a response to the Jansenist heresy. Unfortunately, devotion to the Sacred Heart of Jesus in that era put great accent on self-abnegation and bodily mortifications that sometimes bordered on self-hate or were dangerous to the body's health and safety. This is the opposite of true devotion, in which we love ourselves as God loves us and at the same time let go of our arrogant unruly ego. For instance, in these words of Blessed Claude de la Colombiere (d. 1682), we see a theme of self-sacrifice: "I desire to forget myself and all that has reference to myself, in order to remove the obstacles that might prevent me from entering the divine heart which you open to me....Teach me to sacrifice myself completely." Once we interpret self as ego, his words are more intelligible and offer a healthy recommendation.

St. Francis de Sales (d. 1622) was a bishop who fought the Jansenist "the body is evil" approach. He proposed the alternative of refuge in and devotion to the Sacred Heart of Jesus. He wrote two classic books: *An Introduction to the Devout Life* and *On the Love of God*. During the sixteenth century, St. Francis de Sales and St. Jane de Chantal (d. 1641) urged devotion to the Sacred Heart. Together, they founded the Visitation Nuns, saying that their congregation was indeed "the work of the hearts of Jesus and Mary." St. Jane de Chantal prayed: "May God give us the grace to live and die in the Sacred Heart." St. Francis de Sales prayed: "May God live in my heart for that is what it is made for."

Aspiration out and inspiration in is how divine life flows through us, just as blood flows to and from the heart. According to St. Francis de Sales, God is a heart of divine life granted to us: "Whoever has Jesus in his heart will soon have him in all his outward behavior." In his sermon for Christmas, St. Francis preached: "[In Jesus] the human is divinized and God is humanized so that God, without ceasing to be God, is human and humans, without ceasing to be human, are God." This evokes the mystical—and contemporary—theme of the divine life residing in the hidden life of ourselves.

St. John Eudes (d. 1680) affirmed the inseparability of the divine and the human and the unconditionality of divine love: "Jesus even loves us in our enemies' hearts....I say boldly that Jesus loves us even in hell." This is certainly an example of God not giving up on humans. St. John prayed: "Jesus, how I long for the universe to be transformed into flaming fires of love for you." St. John Eudes saw the Sacred Heart as a furnace of divine love that transforms us in the alchemical way. He wrote *The Sacred Heart of Jesus,* the first book that showed the theological basis of this devotion. Founder of the Congregation of Jesus and Mary, St. John Eudes spread devotion both to the Sacred Heart of Jesus and to the Immaculate Heart of Mary, and was instrumental in the inclusion in the liturgy of a feast of the Sacred Heart of Jesus and of the Immaculate Heart of Mary. This acknowledges the inseparability of the feminine dimension in devotion to the heart of God.

In 1673, a Visitation nun at Paray le Monial in France, St. Margaret Mary (d. 1690) had a vision of Jesus showing her his heart and asking that devotion to it be increased. He said: "My divine heart is so inflamed with love for humanity, and for you in particular, that it can no longer contain within itself the flames of its ardent love, and must spread them through you, and manifest itself to people and enrich them with the precious treasures I will reveal." The fact that the first vision of many happened on December 29 is significant because it is the feast of St. John the Beloved Disciple, who rested his head on Jesus' heart at the Last Supper. Christ was later to say to St. Margaret: "You are the beloved disciple of my Sacred Heart."

The Jesuits, especially Blessed Claude de la Colombiere and John Croiset, supported and followed St. Margaret Mary in spreading devotion to the Sacred Heart. The order is still committed to this apostolate. John Croiset was closely connected to St. Margaret Mary in devising an integral devotion to the Sacred Heart. She wrote ten letters to him and in 1694, he published a book called *The Devotion to the Sacred Heart of Our Lord Jesus Christ.* In an apparition to St. Margaret Mary, Blessed Claude de la Colombiere was referred to by Jesus as "my best friend." These kindly and intimate appellations and revelations place the accent on an *interactive relationship* to Christ as a friend and lover. The purpose of the visions was not to increase the merit of the recipients but to send them as apostles for the spreading of love.

St. Madeleine Sophie Barat (d. 1865) was a strong advocate of the Sacred Heart devotion and founded a congregation of nuns called the Society of the Sacred Heart. For her, continually recalling the presence of God was the essence of the devotion. She realized that it would take her a whole lifetime to contemplate the Sacred Heart of Jesus, and still she would not fully plumb its depths of meaning.

The devotion to the Sacred Heart of Jesus is not limited to Catholicism. There have been books and references in sermons to the Heart of Jesus in other Christian traditions. In 1642, the Puritan Thomas Goodwin published a book about the Sacred Heart that in 1819 was reprinted by John Wesley, the founder of the Methodists.

Jacob Boehme (d. 1624), a Lutheran mystic, wrote in his *Confessions:* "The transformation is of this world. It is not an ascent to another world....The true heaven is everywhere, even where you stand and where you go....This world in its inner core unfolds its properties and powers in union with the heaven aloft and so there is one heart, one Being, one will, one God all in all."

Anglican Neoplatonist mystic Thomas Traherne (d. 1674) describes this magnificent vision: "At his cross we enter the heart of the universe....All the desire wherewith He longs after a returning sinner, makes Him esteem a broken heart....His heart is always abroad in the midst of the earth; seeing and rejoicing in His wonders there....In all thy keeping, keep thy heart, for out of it come the issues of life and death."

Poets access and express mystical themes in their love poetry, and we have already noticed that so many of the mystical revelations speak of experiences that resemble human physical love. There is indeed no distinction of loves in true spirituality. Notice the theme of the exchange of hearts in love poetry. For instance, Sir Philip Sidney in the sixteenth century wrote:

> My true love hath my heart, and I have his,
> By just exchange, one for the other given....
> His heart in me, keeps me and him in one...
> He loves my heart for once it was his own:
> I cherish his, because in me it bides....
> My heart was wounded with his wounded heart....

In our own modern times we read in e.e. cummings:

> i carry your heart with me (I carry it in
> my heart) i am never without it....

Teilhard de Chardin

"We tirelessly and ceaselessly search for Something, we know not what, which will appear in the end to those who have penetrated to the very heart of reality."
—Teilhard de Chardin

Pierre Teilhard de Chardin was a Jesuit paleontologist, naturalist, and mystic who died in 1955. He distinguished between the tangential energy of increasing diversity in nature and the radial energy of increasing "withinness" in nature and in all of us. Evolution occurs as both energies work together, a merger of the natural and the mystical. Teilhard de Chardin saw divine consciousness as the deepest "within," the interior reality of all creation, immanence. In this interiority is an urge to move toward more and more transcendence. The Sacred Heart reveals that the withinness of God is love and that our withinness, our soul, is love too if only we would allow it to become activated.

Teilhard wrote: "We are evolution looking at itself and conscious of itself." Withinness is mirrorlike since it refers to how consciousness becomes aware of itself, as big an event as the arrival of the first atom. Evolution is heading toward ever-deepening withinness. That was Teilhard's luminous metaphor of the Sacred Heart of God in the universe.

Teilhard de Chardin made a significant contribution to the forming of a mature devotion to the Sacred Heart. He rescued it from sentimentality and superstition and integrated it into his electrifying vision of the universe. He described his thrilling and sublime vision of the Sacred Heart in *The Heart of Matter* (Harvest, 1976). Devotion to the Sacred Heart gave Teilhard de Chardin "a sense of the solidity of Christ...the immersion of the divine in the corporeal...a glowing core of fire...able to insinuate itself everywhere...to make love of the cosmic milieu." The

Sacred Heart of Jesus is the alchemical vessel in which fiery transformation happens.

The fire image of the mystics was expanded and enriched by Teilhard within his new cosmology. As we have seen, there are indeed many precedents for this metaphor. *The Gospel of St. Thomas* presents Jesus as saying: "He who nears me nears the heart of the fire." In the Litany of the Sacred Heart is the invocation "Glowing furnace of love." Images of the Sacred Heart show a perpetual flame arising from its center. Fire burns away the selfish ego so that our basic goodness, our true nature as love, can shine through. This is an ancient theme in many religious traditions. The pagan mystic and philosopher Plotinus (d. 270) writes in his *Enneads* VI 9:9: "We all have the vision that may be of him [God] and of ourselves but it is of a self made for splendor, brimful of intellectual light, become that very light, pure, buoyant, unburdened, raised to Godhood…all aflame." The fire in the heart of God is the same fire that burns in us once we have the interior vision that lets us acknowledge divinity within ourselves and then design our lives accordingly.

When St. Paul says that "our God is a consuming fire," we see again a metaphor for the dismantling of ego-centeredness. Christ's heart can become the fiery center of ourselves, and in that alchemical blaze the ego is transformed to the gold of humility and generosity. Our spiritual practice is thus to turn our ego energy into compassion for others, not at the cost of personal esteem, but as a fruit of it. This prayer of St. Margaret Mary states the connection well: "O divine fire…consume me and I will not resist.…Your lively flames make those live who die in them.…I adore you most Sacred Heart of Jesus. Inflame my heart with the divine love with which your own is all on fire." Fire is associated with hell but in the context of mystical revelations, fire is about love. The Sacred Heart is a divine pledge that the world will not end by fire but be reborn in it.

For the ancient Greeks and Egyptians healing was caused by light and fire. This may best resemble Teilhard's mystical sense of the fire of the Sacred Heart that brings light and healing to the world. This same fire is a light within us that lets us see through the gross appearances in the world to the transpersonal life deep within all things. Teilhard was blessed with that kind of vision. Virginia Woolf tells of it in *The Waves:* "Things are losing their hardness; now even my body lets the light through." In *The Dark Night of the Soul,* St. John of the Cross writes similarly: "I went out into the world with no other light except the one that was burning in my heart." The Upanishads say: "A self-luminous being resides in the lotus of the heart, surrounded by the senses, and is the Light of our intelligence." We keep noticing similar realizations in all traditions, confirming a collective truth.

On Pentecost, the apostles and Mary gathered in their grief; Jesus was gone from their midst yet at the same time they trusted that he was risen. The Holy Spirit then came upon them in tongues of fire. Fire follows grief and trust, two hallmarks of personal relationships and of our spiritual life too. We grieve our failings, our losses, and our wounds. The fire of zeal to share the good news happened to Mary and the apostles in the context of these human predicaments. They brought to others the fruits of their own life story, and the grace of fire from the Spirit of love opened it in a new way.

Teilhard wrote:

> Throughout my life, through my life, the world has, little by little, caught fire in my sight until, aflame all around me, it has become almost completely luminous from within....Such has been my experience in contact with the earth, the diaphany of the divine at the heart of the universe on fire....Christ, his heart a fire, capable of penetrating everywhere, and gradually, spreading everywhere....Our spiritual being is

continually nourished by the countless energies of the
tangible world.

Teilhard goes on to show his trust in the mystical power of
the natural world: "No power in the world can prevent us from
savoring [the world's] joys because it happens at a level deeper
than any power; and no power in the world, for the same reason,
can compel it to appear." Teilhard even goes so far as to admit:
"If, as the result of some interior revolution, I were to lose in succession my faith in Christ, my faith in a personal God, and my
faith in spirit, I feel that I should continue to believe invincibly in
the world. The world…is the first, the last, and the only thing in
which I believe. It is by this faith that I live."

For Teilhard de Chardin, the cosmic Christ was born from
the Sacred Heart:

> Under the symbol of the Sacred Heart the divine
> assumed for me, the form of fire….[T]hrough its
> power to become universal this fire proved able to
> invade and impregnate with love the whole atmos-
> phere of the world in which I lived….It is in the
> Sacred Heart that the conjunction of the divine and
> the cosmic has taken place….There lies the power that
> from the beginning has attracted and conquered
> me….All the later development of my interior life has
> been nothing other than the evolution of that seed.

In *Toward the Future,* Teilhard wrote: "Someday, after mas-
tering the winds, the waves, the tides, and gravity, we will harness
for God the energies of love. And then, for the second time,
humankind will have discovered fire." The discovery that love is
the essence of evolution is the equivalent in importance of
humanity as finding fire and learning to generate it and use it.

The Sacred Heart is a promise that the universe is converging toward love.

Teilhard wrote of a noosphere, a term he coined to describe a layer of thought-consciousness in the universe. Perhaps there is also a cardiosphere, a realm of ever-increasing heart in the cosmos. Teilhard in fact said: "The great secret, the great mystery, is this: there is a heart of the world and this heart is the heart of Christ." In the Sacred Heart of Jesus he discovered a way to find the absolute in the tangible, the radial in the tangential, to use his terms. The materialization of divine love became the meaning of the Sacred Heart in his life. His mystical vision showed him that the Sacred Heart is the sacrality of the cosmos.

Teilhard de Chardin saw evolution as feminine and Christ as masculine energy culminating in the Sacred Heart. His devotion to and comprehension of the connection of the Sacred Heart to evolution developed throughout his life. In 1916 he wrote how the Heart of Jesus fills the whole world; that is, love fills the world. This Sacred Heart was not only the love of Jesus for humanity but also a unifying force upholding the universe. The world happens because of love. In 1940 Teilhard journaled: "The Sacred Heart is the personal heart of the cosmos...the motor of evolution." The cosmic Christ came to him as "an expansion of the heart of Jesus." In 1950 he added: "The Sacred Heart is the heart of the heart of the world, the center of the center of the universe." In letters to his mother, who instilled the devotion in him in his early life, Teilhard used phrases like these: "communion with the desires of the Sacred Heart"..."universal center of the convergent universe." Quotations like these from Teilhard de Chardin show how devotion to the Sacred Heart was, for him, a firm commitment to social and evolutionary change.

All this became one focus for Teilhard de Chardin: a fascination with matter and an adoration of Christ, a God of flesh and blood alive in the Eucharist. For him, there was a unity in the forward movement of evolution and upwardly moving desire for transcendence. In this sense Teilhard showed how desire helps us move on since our longings for a better future evince it into being. The Heart of Christ is the Omega, now seen in our new perspective not as a finality but as an ever-unfolding opening. Indeed, the universe does not so much have a goal as a direction toward greater diversity and deeper communion.

Teilhard stated many times that "union differentiates" so we become more ourselves as we relate more to others. In fact, the fullness of our being is not personal consciousness but interpersonal and ultimately transpersonal consciousness; that is, tangential energy becoming radial energy. We do not lose ourselves as we move toward interrelatedness. We only lose our sense of separation. For Teilhard, the triune nature of God reflects this same reality of interconnection. The Trinity refers to three Persons in one God. "The word *person* in Greek does not mean "self" as we denote an individual self. *Person* means "being-in-relationship." There is no such thing as an individual self in the Trinity, only a *perichoresis*, an interrelatedness. The Trinity is indeed the essential reality of all interrelatedness. To appreciate the Trinity, we need an experience of God as community, and this happens best when we are creating community here and now.

For Teilhard de Chardin evolution is gradual interpersonalization. The destiny of all creation is intercommunion, exactly what happens when Jesus offers us his heart in holy communion. An ever-evolving interdependence corresponds to what in ecology is the undivided web of life. The cosmos is a field of energies, structured in an organized way, and relying on continual exchanges and interdependencies. To cherish and contribute to that exchange by ecological awareness and action is devotion to the Heart of Jesus since the heart of the cosmos is his.

Humans have a natural instinct for self-preservation but that will not help the planet survive. For that we need an instinct for planetary-preservation and that is not built in. It takes the spiritual practice of loving-kindness applied to nature. Once our heart is open as the Sacred Heart is, our caring includes all beings. Open means universal in reach. Devotion to the Sacred Heart of Jesus opens our ecological consciousness.

Focus penetrates illusion and gives a clear vision of reality. Teilhard de Chardin focused on the image of the Sacred Heart: "Jesus, I love you for the extensions of your body and soul to the farthest corners of creation through grace, through life, and through matter....I love you as a world, as this world, which has captivated my heart. And it is you, I now realize, that my fellow humans, even those who do not believe, sense and seek throughout the magic immensities of the cosmos."

Karl Rahner

In love, the gates of my soul spring open, allowing me to breathe a new air of freedom and forget my own petty self. In love, my whole being streams forth out of the rigid confines of narrowness and self-assertion that make me a prisoner of my own poverty and emptiness.—Karl Rahner

Another important contributor to the maturation of the devotion to the Sacred Heart of Jesus was German Jesuit theologian Karl Rahner. He saw the Sacred Heart as a symbol of surrender to the divine will. He reframed the concept of our need to make reparation to Christ. In his view, we do not *make* reparation. We participate in reparation *already made* once for all by Christ. "Reparations are...rehearsals of the believing and willing heart for its allotted share in the fate of our Lord...(the fate reserved in the world for his love)...who as the Lamb of God takes away the sins of the world." To choose to suffer in more ways than life presents to us is to question the efficacy of Christ's once-for-all sacrifice. In Jesus' time, the priests in the temple in Jerusalem performed sacrifices to accomplish forgiveness for the sins of the people. Jesus saw that as no longer necessary because he himself was the final sacrifice: the Lamb of God. Rahner clarifies it in this way: "Our Lord's love enters into the history of this sinful world and wins its victory by enduring unto death the sins of the world and its own rejection by sinful men. All this outpouring of love is a revelation of his heart." This forgiving love is reminiscent of the loving-kindness of the father of the prodigal son. The father was on the lookout always for his wayward son and he ran to embrace him *before* the son apologized for his misdeeds.

Rahner also commented on the traditional view that we are called to console the suffering Christ. He reconfigures it as "not as a sympathetic wish to console but as a generous and unselfish willingness to accept the law of Christ's life, the law of voluntary self-sacrifice." Comments like this free us from a sentimental style of devotion and open us to risk living in the likeness of Christ. This does not remove or reduce the soothing quality of the Sacred Heart of Jesus. *The comforting power is now in alignment with Christ's way of living and many graces flow from that commitment. This is how devotion combines comfort and challenge, both so necessary for a true religious spirit.*

Christian mystics saw the wounded heart of Jesus as an open door into an initiation into the interior life. This is the paradox of a wound as a source of grace. It helps us see why voluntary sacrifice has been so much a part of religious and patriotic history. Roman writer Apuleius describes a fellow devotee of Osiris: "His left foot was wounded so he walked with a hobble…a clear sign of the will of the gods." Also in ancient times, a wound was one of the credentials of a guide for the initiation process. Christian initiation makes suffering an entry into the life of grace.

The medieval fascination with Christ's passion made asceticism, often extreme and bodily harmful, seem like a path of merit. Our more mature view recognizes suffering as legitimate when it is a sacrifice of ourselves for others (self-sacrifice) or an endurance of the conditions of existence over which we have no control. We bear the suffering that is a given of our human life but we are not called to self-inflict abuse. We gain nothing by whipping ourselves as St. Francis did, and even he, on his deathbed, in answer to the question "Do you have any regrets?"— said, "Yes, one, I was too hard on Brother Ass."

I recall in my childhood a prayer to the Sacred Heart of Jesus: "Jesus, give me a heart of steel toward myself, a heart of flesh toward others, and a heart of fire for God." Now we understand that the great mystery of the Sacred Heart is in how to have compassion, a heart of flesh, *toward oneself* and not only toward others. This is the opposite of—and remedy for—self-loathing. The loving-kindness we see in the Sacred Heart is meant to be shown to ourselves as well as to others. In a philosophical voice, we hear Friedrich Nietzsche warn: "We see an insanity of the will that is without parallel: man's will to find himself guilty, and unredeemably so." In the divine voice, we hear: "A new heart I will give you, and a new spirit I will put within you; and I will remove from your body the heart of stone and give you a heart of flesh" (Ezek 36:26).

St. Paul in Colossians 1:24 says: "In my flesh I complete what is lacking in Christ's afflictions for the sake of his body, that is, the church." What is "lacking" does not imply deficiency on Christ's part but offers us a role in redemption with him. We do not make reparation to him but we join him in what, in Jewish tradition, is called *tikkun olam*, the repair of the world. The Sacred Heart of Jesus is the final clue to who we really are, love, and what we are here for: *tikkun*, to repair, build, and *cocreate* the world from love into love. Devotion to the Sacred Heart is the spiritual practice of repairing the world in that loving way. We have consciousness, virtue, and inventiveness so we can mend the world that shadow-forces attempt to demolish. This is how we, as cocreators, continue what God has begun; and how we continue, as coredeemers, the work Christ has accomplished. The word *redeem* comes from a Latin word referring to the freeing of a slave. Redemption is finding our freedom to love in loveless surroundings so that love becomes the law of humankind, as it already is the intent and purpose of the universe: "in Christ Jesus our Lord, in whom we have access to God in boldness and confidence through faith in him" (Eph 3:12). The Heart of Jesus is then the heart of the world and the driving force of evolution precisely in Dante's sense: "Love steers the stars and other planets."

Rahner understood the Sacred Heart of Jesus to be a profound symbol of the mystery of being loved by God *personally*. The core of our being is love, an abiding reality in all of us. Love of one another, loving-kindness toward one another, *is* devotion to the Sacred Heart. To repeat Rahner's words quoted in chapter 2: "The divine love of the Eternal Word has become incarnate in the human love of Christ. It has fashioned itself a place in history and cast itself for an unmistakable role in the sinful world. Thereby it has guaranteed that love, and not righteous anger, is God's first and last message to the world." The Sacred Heart of Jesus means that God is not retaliatory but unceasingly merciful no matter what we do.

Rahner also understood the reversal of values that a spiritual life demands from us:

> Every person must live, irrespective of whether he decides for or against Christianity, in a situation marked by the outward, and therefore also inward, absence of God, a situation which corresponds to Golgotha and Gethsemane in the life of Jesus, where life is to be found in death, where abandonment

implies the deepest proximity to God, and where the power of God parades itself in weakness.

The Sacred Heart of Jesus tells us what divine love is really about. As Alfred North Whitehead wrote: "The best image of God's nature is that of tender care that will not be lost." Pope Pius XI referred to the Sacred Heart as *"Totius religionis summa"*: the summation of all that religion means. Institutional religion is often about its own preservation. Authentic religion is meant to offer only one thing: a technology for loving with tender care.

Prayers

We sought through prayer and meditation to improve our conscious contact with God, as we understood him, praying only for knowledge of his will for us and the power to carry that out. —Step Eleven of Alcoholics Anonymous

Jesus of my heart, I ask for this grace: to seek you in prayer and meditation so that my conscious contact and communion with you may increase.

To seek you in prayer and meditation means that I give up my attachment to worldly values: I give up making any person, any amount of money, any status or position, or any form of addiction into a god, a higher power.

As I feel my communion with you increasing I notice that I love others more than ever.

I ask only for knowledge of your will for me and the ability to carry that out in my daily life.

Jesus, I am committing myself to accepting the things in life I cannot change and I ask for the grace of serenity.

I am committing myself to changing the things in life I *can* change and I ask for the grace of courage.

I am committing myself to knowing the difference and I ask for the grace of wisdom.

This is my way of entering and cherishing a mystical relationship with your heart.

Jesus, take away the arrogance in my ego and give me your heart in its place. Take away my ego-centeredness and make your heart and its purposes the center of myself.

I willingly enter the fire of your heart and let your heart burn away my ego and enflame me with enthusiasm for the conversion of the world to the desires of your heart.

I feel the passionate longing of your heart for all humanity and I ask to be an apostle of your love.

I want to be your friend as you are mine.

I want to make friends with the world and bring your friendship to the world.

Jesus, I feel you as an ongoing and never-failing companion with me on my journey through life.

At the same time, sometimes I lose my sense of contact with you.

Let me hold in each hand, all at once, both "Why hast thou forsaken me?" and "Thou art with me."

Then I can walk through the valley of the shadow of death with you beside me and in me.

I can experience the dark isolation and trust your presence even when I do not *feel* it.

You felt all this on the cross and you are my companion in it now whether or not I notice it.

This is how I show you my faith and I am thankful for the grace of having it.

I have faith in your heart being faithful to me and to all of us in this valley of delights and distresses.

I ask for an awakening and when it happens I ask to share this faith in your abiding presence with those who do not yet know you.

May I always remain loyal to those who are still lost in the ever-darkening sunset of hate, greed, and delusion.

I consecrate my life to joining you in letting the light through.

I found myself asking myself, is this what life is for, to burn it up in sweating, steaming, and toiling in a race for power, prestige, passion, pleasure and piles of stocks and bonds, from every one of which I am going to be separated some day? —James Fox, abbot of Gethsemani, to his classmates at Harvard at their 25th reunion

Chapter Five

SHOWING OUR DEVOTION

"Come to me, all you that are weary and are carrying heavy burdens, and I will give you rest. Take my yoke upon you, and learn from me; for I am gentle and humble in heart, and you will find rest for your souls. For my yoke is easy, and my burden is light."

—Matthew 11:28–30

The four elements all religions have in common are belief, morality, ritual, and devotion. Each of the four is meant to be experiential and each applies to devotion to the Sacred Heart of Jesus:

We *believe* in the promise that we will never lose our capacity to love no matter what happens to us or how we are treated.

We act with *moral* rectitude, generous love, virtue, and conviction. Morality includes universal compassion and work for world justice not just personally ethical behavior.

We engage in *rituals* or *sacraments* that enact Christ consciousness and grant us access to special graces. Faith is belief in a transcendent reality. Rituals make it possible for us to *feel* this reality. This is how rituals help us build our faith.

We experience *devotion,* a personal loving relationship with God. Devotion makes mystical experience available to everyone.

Devotion is how we come to know God in a personal way, how God becomes personal.

Devotion to the Sacred Heart in medieval times was found mostly among mystics. Thanks to the revelations to St. Margaret Mary and the zeal of her French Jesuit helpers, the devotion became universal in the church. In our own parochial school experience, we may recall the accent on receiving communion on nine first Fridays to assure that we would not someday die without the last anointing. It seemed a sure thing since it placed a hold on God. Karl Rahner remarks that promises from the Sacred Heart, based on the visions of St. Margaret Mary, are not to be construed as "a recipe for gaining a hold over God." Note, in any case, that "the promises" were assembled and based on her visions but not specifically vocalized by Jesus to her. As we grow in spiritual consciousness, we move away from superstitions that seem to assure a stranglehold on God. *The only promise of the Sacred Heart of Jesus is that we have not yet lost nor will we ever lose our capacity to love.* This is because of the good news that the core of us is the *cor* (heart) of God.

The accent on the promises also reflected the belief, more in evidence in the past, that salvation is focused on how each individual can be rewarded with heaven. Now, since Vatican II, we have a much wider perspective. We see that we are here as a community, each with individual gifts and paths, but all members of one mystical body, one earth. We are here to care about one another and contribute to the evolution of all of us toward spiritual consciousness. We are members of a church community called to build a kingdom of peace and justice on this planet and to confront the powers of exploitation or violence, and of the corporate, personal, or political greed that subverts that possibility. With this new sense of mission, our devotional life changes. The accent is no longer on formulated prayers and devotional practices to gain merit for ourselves. Though these have a place, they are secondary to our major purpose as Christians: to join the purposes of the Sacred Heart of Jesus. His purposes are to bring loving-kindness into human relationships, and to establish a kingdom of justice, peace, and love here on earth for every person and for the whole world. Devotion, like salvation, is personal, and yet it is communally conscious. Huston Smith says: "We are embodied souls; we have to act on our faith."

The Eucharist: Centerpiece of Devotion to the Sacred Heart

Where was Jesus looking when he said: "This is my Body?"
—Basil Matthews

The early church chose the word *ekklesia* to describe itself. This word meant citizenry, which was expanded to include all individuals, even women and slaves. It is significant that they did not choose the word *koinon,* which means guild; that is, a group with one specific interest. The church was meant to be universal in its inclusiveness, without class distinctions or rankings: "There is no longer Jew or Greek, there is no longer slave or free, there is no longer male and female; for all of you are one in Christ Jesus" (Gal 3:28). Catholic means "universal" in that the outreach is without discrimination or border. This is evangelical Catholicism. In mystical Catholicism, universal means in-reach to a center by the whole human community. That center is not some physical place like Rome. It is the Eucharist which, according to theologian Henri de Lubac, makes the church.

The Sacred Heart as well as the Eucharist show that the boundary between spirit and matter is not as clear-cut as we might have imagined. As Teilhard de Chardin wrote to Christ:

From the moment that you said "This is my Body," not only the bread on the altar, but to a certain extent everything in the universe became yours and now nourishes in our souls the life of grace and the spirit....All the communions of all men, present, past, and future are one communion....Right from the hands that knead the dough to the hands that consecrate it, only one Host is being formed....The Host is formed by the totality of the world and all the duration of time is needed for its consecration....Over every living thing which is to spring up, to grow, to flower, to ripen during this day, say again the words: "This is my Body." Over every death force which is waiting to corrode, wither, or cut down, speak again your command: "This is my Blood."

Carl Jung comments in this same respect: "The symbols of the Mass penetrate into the deepest layers of the psyche and of its history....The mystery of the Eucharist transforms the soul of the person, only partial, into a totality symbolically expressed by Christ. In this sense, we can speak of the Mass as the rite of the individuation process."

Alchemy reverses values and combines opposites and, in that sense, it is like mysticism. The alchemical or the paradoxical theme in the Eucharist is that the least valued, nutritionless bread becomes the most valuable, all-nourishing food of the soul. *The Eucharist presents us with the good news that something behind mortal appearances is personal and loves us.* This reversal of common sense in favor of divine meaning is visible only when we see with faith. The Eucharist is the means by which we become intimate with God. Good-byes are intimate and the Eucharist was given to us as a parting gift at the Last Supper. It was how Jesus found a way to stay with us. Only a lover would have cared for us in that way. Only one who knew what it felt like to be forsaken would have appreciated how we needed the ongoing presence and full accessibility of his heart for all our lives. This is how the Eucharist is the mystical presence of the Sacred Heart. St. Augustine says: "The body of Christ gives the body of Christ to the body of Christ." The presence is therefore in the community. The Eucharist has only taken effect in us when we are community and when no one is excluded from our concern, respect, and compassion. Then the Eucharist, like the Sacred Heart, is a verb, an action of universal, limitless, borderless love in community. The Great Amen at the end of the canon of the Mass is a yes not only to the presence of Christ in the Eucharist but to his presence in all of us gathered to celebrate him.

We are the sacraments—the visible signs of the unity of God's people—of the Blessed Sacrament. We are the way the Eucharist comes to life as consecrated hosts that are here to nourish the sufferings and joys of the world. Since childhood, our destiny was always visible in the monstrance holding the host, the heart of our faith. Our destiny is perpetual exposition of our love for all to see and share. The design of devotional life is unique to each of us while at the same time a communal event in the believing community. This is how we become the benediction of the eucharistic Heart of Jesus. Nothing less is asked of us; nothing less is offered to us. When we imagine we can prepare for the Eucharist by making ourselves worthy, we miss its gift dimension.

Sacramentum in ancient Rome referred to an oath. The Eucharist and all the sacraments are the resources for our commitment or oath to resist the dominant paradigm. We act with love in season and out of season till more and more hearts are converted to the radical loving-kindness Christ showed by his life and gives us now by his grace. Our sacramental life then becomes an enthusiastic devotedness to Christ's mission in the world. Jesus is the exemplar of the virtues by which we fulfill ourselves. He communicates this in the Gospels and in mystical revelations throughout the history of the church.

The Practice of Devotedness

The following authentic devotional practices are based on Gospel and mystical teachings that reflect the qualities of Jesus.

• *Engaging in Prayer and Presence.* We grow in consciousness of Jesus' presence in our daily life and form a prayerful connection to him throughout the day. We combine personal prayer, liturgical life, and contemplation. We do not limit prayer to words. We appreciate the importance of silence for recollecting and replenishing ourselves. At the same time, silence is so powerful a tool to release us from ego-centeredness that in the silence we hear more clearly the cries of the world. This is how silent contemplation leads to compassion.

• *Making Amends.* We repent for how we have hurt or excluded others from our love. We repent our greed, hate, retaliations, dishonesty, lying, indifference, and so on. We repent any complicity in the policies of violence happening in our country. We repent our disregard of Christ and his teachings. We make amends for each of these lapses from grace. We ask forgiveness and resolve to change our way of living so that it aligns more perfectly with the virtues of Jesus.

• *Being Eucharist.* We frequent the Eucharist as a gift from, and a receiving of, the heart of Christ. We see how in the Eucharist we extend and appreciate Christ's risen body through matter, in matter, and as matter. We keep looking for ways to be in communion with the desires of the Sacred Heart by being in communion with all humanity. This is the result of participating in the Eucharist. We know it has taken effect when our minds become utterly free of bias and our hearts become lovingly inclusive of all people: "In that renewal there is no longer Greek and Jew, circumcised and uncircumcised, barbarian, Scythian, slave and free; but Christ is all and in all!" (Col 3:11).

• *Showing Unconditional Love.* We make a commitment to show unconditional love and universal compassion in any way we can. In every place and circumstance we extend loving-kindness to every person. This means never giving up on anyone even those who run from our love or who have hurt us. The appearance of the Sacred Heart of Jesus over and over in the history of Christianity promises clearly: "It is never too late to love." The former devotion emphasized how Jesus loves us. Now we focus also on how we can love others as he loves us. We practice this love not as compulsive caretaking but as sane dedication. We love without measure, without distinction of persons, without limit. We increase our capacity to forgive rather than retaliate when others fail us. We are no longer prejudiced. We want all people to be free to be who they are. Our love is utterly inclusive, as big as Jesus' Heart. Our lifelong biases vanish and we live from the heart. To see and hear others from a heart place means without judgment, hate, or criticism. We speak our truth but not in ways that hurt or condemn others.

• *Loving Ourselves and Letting Go of Ego.* We foster an unconditional love for ourselves too. We give up self-loathing and appreciate ourselves as heirs of the Sacred Heart, the unconditionally deepest core of ourselves. Jesus, in the Gospel, asks us to learn from him because he is "gentle and humble in heart" (Matt 11:29). Every time we work on reducing the importance of ego, with all its arrogant self-centeredness, we are showing devotion to the Sacred Heart and appreciating our inner self, the indwelling Spirit. To let go of ego is to exchange ego for Jesus' heart. This includes abandoning our obsession with self-importance, acquisition, and control. Indeed, controlling is seeking security in ourselves. When we rely on controlling, we lose our belief in grace. Controlling, in the divine value system will mean seeking our security only in the heart of Christ. Giving will come to mean more than having.

Forgiveness will mean more to us than retaliating. Love will mean more than anything.

- *Practicing a Bodily Devotion.* There is no dualism in authentic spirituality. Spirituality does not exclude or minimize the body. "He assumed me wholly...to save the whole. What was not assumed was not healed," says St. John Damascene. Our core self is embodied and our heart is the center of our physical self. Devotion to the Sacred Heart is meant to be a bodily devotion. The image of the Sacred Heart is indeed so physical a devotion as to convey the fact that the body is a worthy means of love and a suitable object of love. This is in opposition to the implicit Monophysite heresy still prevalent among some Christians. The Monophysites believed that Christ was only divine and not truly human. John McDade, SJ, writes: "You can't have Christianity without being drawn into a mysticism about how *Christ's body becomes the body of redeemed sinners and the locus of their salvation,* precisely the mystery symbolized by devotion to the Sacred Heart" [emphasis by McDade]. St. Paul expressed it to the Colossians: "And you, who were once estranged and hostile in mind, doing evil deeds, he has now reconciled *in the body of his flesh* through death" (Col 1:21–2; emphasis added).

We show our devotion bodily when we appreciate our body as a worthy means of love and an object of love, like the body of Christ, the mystical body of redeemed humanity. We are unafraid of emotional and bodily responsiveness as a feature of devotion and ritual. A bodily devotion includes all the senses as well as ritual items, candles, incense, images, and more, as appropriate features of devotion. As humans, we are both rational and animal. Spirituality has wrongly been equated with focus on the rational, the immaterial, the nonearthly, and the nonbodily. Actually, spirituality includes the body in every religious tradition except in those that have a fear of the shadow side of us, of sex, of nature, or of the feminine. Teilhard de Chardin connects a consciousness of our personal body to that of the physical universe:

> Christ invests himself organically with the very majesty of his creation. And it is in no way metaphorical to say that man finds himself capable of experiencing and discovering his God in the whole length, breadth, and depth of the world in movement. To be able to say literally to God that one loves him, not only with all one's body, all one's heart, and all one's soul, but with every fiber of the unifying universe, that is a prayer that can only be made in space-time.

By baptism we are called then to transubstantiate matter into spirit.

• *Exchanging Hearts.* We contemplate ourselves in an exchange of hearts with Jesus. He takes our selfishness and gives back generosity; he takes our fears and gives back love; he takes our arrogant ego and gives us back his own Self. The exchange of hearts means that Jesus wants us to come to him and that we can trade our dark shadow side for the bright side of humanity we saw in his life.

• *Saying Yes to Life's Givens.* We appreciate the predicaments and conditions of our mortality as challenges and gifts from the Heart of Jesus, open wide so all the givens of existence can find a place in it and through it. Things happen to us so we can grow and become more compassionate. *The events and twists of our lives are not arrows from a punitive God but rays of light from a divine life in and around us.* Since God acts in mysterious, illogical ways, union with God is simply assent to those ways; that is, to the conditions of existence. Yes to life's givens is a high form of reverence for God. Mystic St. Teresa of Avila wrote: "When we accept what happens to us and make the best of it, we are praising God." Then we are most like the incarnate Son, within and, at the same time, above the conditions and contingencies of existence. Our unconditional yes is transportation to transcendence in that we behold the whole rather than being blinded by the limited. Devotional assent is not just accepting the conditions of existence but becoming thankful for them and cooperating with them. This is aligning ourselves with the love by which all things are coming together to bring about the good. This love grows in us by spiritual practice and comes to us as a grace. We learn to love better when we say, "Yes, now what?" rather than, "Why me?" *Yes* is "Thy will be done," and as Dante says, "His will is our peace." *Why* is stress and pain; a questioning rather than a trusting.

• *Trusting That Everything Is Grace:* We see all we do and can do as graces to be thankful for, not as accomplishments of our ego operating on its own power. We keep finding ways to join our ego effort to the workings of grace in us. All that happens is our path. All that happens is the good news that "God so loved the world" that he made all things to be so many means of grace. Everything that happens to us; every person we meet; every event and challenge we face; every thought, word, and action we think and say and do—all of this is a ray of grace from the Sacred Heart. We consciously acknowledge this as we did in the Morning Offering in our childhood prayers. Here is a new morning offering that can be prayed throughout the day:

> Jesus, I say yes thankfully for everything that
> happens to me today
> as a gift from your heart
> and as an opportunity to give and receive love.
> I dedicate all that I think, say, feel, and do
> to the loving purposes of your heart.

• *Taking Refuge.* To find refuge is to turn to something in times of woe or fear and discover in it a sense of containment and safety so that we can face what ails or scares us. We enter the

Sacred Heart of Jesus for refuge, rather than our usual places of refuge that are so often forms of addiction. This reflects the mystical theme of the Sacred Heart as a source of solace: "I will give you rest."

• *Choosing New Values.* Jesus says: "Do not think that I have come to abolish the law or the prophets; I have come not to abolish but to fulfill" (Matt 5:17). A Latin word for "fulfill," *implere,* became the English word *implement.* We make decisions that implement Christian values in how we handle money, ambition, life choices, and our relationships to other humans and to nature. We become more politically aware and continually find ways to bring our sense of justice to bear on changing public life for the better. This is establishing the kingdom of God on earth as it is in heaven. We are not then surprised when the fate exacted by the world for living Christ's love becomes our fate. At the same time, we do not knowingly inflict suffering on ourselves as if self-torture were meritorious. Jesus wanted to gather a group of exiles from the dominant culture to become a prophetic voice to that culture and its institutions that have joined it. This plan recapitulates the Jewish exile in Babylon. It is also reminiscent of the statement of Jesus that he had nowhere to lay his head. This is a metaphor of exile, of being without the standard nests and holes in which we hide when we rely on worldly powers to protect us. To stand against the greed and violence of our culture is to become an exile, alone in no-man's-land. That is, of course, the exact location of the pure land of the kingdom of God.

• *Honoring the Heart of Mary.* Our devotion extends to the heart of Mary and acknowledges the role of the mother and the feminine in our spirituality. "As truly as God is our father so truly is God our mother," wrote the mystic Juliana of Norwich.

• *Consecrating Ourselves.* On June 11, 1899, Pope Leo XIII solemnly consecrated all humankind to the Sacred Heart of Jesus. We revive that moment by consecrating ourselves to an unconditional love for the world. We vow dedication to the salvation of all beings. We pray that all leaders and all people may be converted to the life of enlightened love. Then we can say not only that "God so loved the world that he gave his only Son" (John 3:16) but also that he sent everyone of us as sons and daughters to join in his redemptive work.

• *Honoring the Image.* We appreciate the image of the Sacred Heart as a mystical vision, keeping it in our living space and/or in our consciousness. We see the image of the Sacred Heart not as an object above us but as a mirror of what our own hearts look like when we open ourselves to love: "A new heart I will give you, and a new spirit I will put within you" (Ezek 36:26). We are always free to form our own image of the Sacred Heart and cherish it within ourselves. The image does not have to be external nor does it have to match either the traditional or modern versions we have seen. It is also appropriate that the image may change as we age and enter new phases of life—and even that we may go beyond images altogether.

• *Making a Pilgrimage.* According to Huston Smith there are four common aspects to pilgrimage in the history of religion: singleness of purpose, freedom from distraction, ordeal or penance, and offerings. We can show devotion by visiting a shrine of Jesus or Mary that is far enough away to give us a sense of a journey that expresses these four qualities. In addition, we might notice if we are called to a pilgrimage to those who suffer because of illness, famine, or any form of exploitation. We can join or follow the example of groups like Doctors Without Borders, the Peace Corps, or of individuals like Mother Theresa as we reach out to those in need. *This is a visit to Jesus in person:* "Truly I tell you, just as you did it to one of the least of these who are members of my family, you did it to me" (Matt 25:40).

• *Bringing Light.* We seek ways to deepen our sense of our role on the planet as God's fire. We burn away the ignorance and violence in our own egos. We ignite the forces of evolutionary love. We bring light to the world. We are fractals of divine light, beams radiating from Jesus the "light of the world." We are here today because divine light wants to refract and illumine the world in the unique way each of us is gifted to show it. We see a loving intent in the universe: that intent is the Sacred Heart of the cosmos.

• *Spreading the Devotion.* We are eager to share the joy of devotion to the Sacred Heart. Our devotedness overflows and we persuade not as much by words as by example. Our evangelical challenge is to awaken a relationship in others so that they know Jesus as they will or can know him. This is what Meister Eckhart called "the birth of Christ in us." We can describe the gospel message from the words of the scriptures. But an intimate relationship with Jesus is a spiritually and bodily felt sense that cannot be fully communicated or defined. The best we can do in spreading devotion to the Sacred Heart of Jesus is to show so much love that others look for the heart that animates it.

The Practice of Loving-Kindness

The human psyche is both individual and collective. The mystical body of Christ is the equivalent of the collective life of humanity. Personal devotion to the Sacred Heart of Jesus, the heart of the mystical body of humanity, therefore always includes consciousness of the world and its needs. Our prayers are never for ourselves alone, as we are not selves alone, but for humanity too, as we are both personal and collective beings. Loving-kindness is a practice that makes this connectedness come to life. The Sacred Heart of Jesus is a powerful and palpable symbol of loving-kindness.

The practice of loving-kindness consists of sending or granting love, compassion, joy, and equanimity to ourselves, to those we love, to those toward whom we are indifferent, to those with whom we have difficulties or who are enemies, and finally to all people everywhere. We begin by asking for the four immeasurable graces—love, compassion, joy, and equanimity—from the Sacred Heart. We express gratitude as we see ourselves becoming more loving, compassionate, joyful, and acceptant of "fortune's buffets and rewards with equal thanks," as Hamlet describes equanimity (*Hamlet:* Act III; Scene ii).

In loving-kindness we ask for the four graces for ourselves first and then for others. The fact that the practice of loving-kindness begins with a love of oneself reminds us that it is not selfish to love ourselves. Friendliness toward oneself is an appropriate place for love to begin. The Sacred Heart of Jesus shows this clearly: in the exchange of hearts, Jesus offers us his love for himself to us. Meister Eckhart tells us: "In giving us his love, God has given us the Holy Spirit so that we can love him with the love with which he loves himself." St. Augustine says: "In the end there will be one Christ loving himself in all his members." To say we are not lovable to ourselves is to say God is wrong in finding us lovable. It is also a denial of the second great commandment: "to love our neighbors *as we love ourselves.*"

A spirituality of heart means that we treat ourselves with gentleness and nurturance. Aristotle wrote: "The heart is...the soul's ability to nourish itself." Friendliness toward oneself helps exile the "SS" from one's life: self-sabotage. We are letting go of hating ourself and of falling prey to our inner critic. *Instead of the critical voice that puts us down, Christ now speaks within us in his own "gentle and humble of heart," encouraging words.* As Meister Eckhart says: "The heavenly Father is my true father and I am his Son. I am identically his son and no other, because the Father does only one kind of thing, making no distinctions. Thus it is that I am his only begotten Son." This is a revolutionary reevaluation of one-self. It is also a mystical realization that we—and all beings—are divinely loving in our core; that is, have a sacred heart of inerad-icable goodness.

Loving-kindness also means friendly love of others in com-passionate, caring, and kind ways. Compassion is not to be thought of as a duty. It wants to happen. The heart automatically responds to pain compassionately. We can override this inclina-tion with layers of ego such as control, criticism, envy, attachment to an outcome, vindictive rejoicing in others' pain, or fear of hav-ing to become gentle, generous, or loving toward others or even toward ourselves.

St. Teresa of Avila found a way to feel compassion toward others: "I shape my heart like theirs and theirs like mine." This is the practice of walking in another's shoes. We look for ways to understand how others feel and we begin to see the pain or fear that may lurk behind some of their behavior. Then it is easier to respond with love rather than with indifference or hate.

The mystery of redemption is that God *joins* us in our suffer-ing. Loving-kindness is *our* way of joining others in their suffering by acknowledging that the pain we feel here and now is identical to that being felt by others in the world, and we join them with compassion and a prayer for mutual healing. *When I suffer with a sense of solidarity with others who are suffering in the way I am, I am offering my suffering to help them. This is a form of prayer.*

Loving-kindness means beaming love, happiness, and the serene light of Christ's kingdom to all beings. This can convert the world and all beings to Christ. We are praying, not prosely-tizing, since we use the practice silently. Loving-kindness means we never give up on others but always trust that Jesus has a way of loving that wins over, transforms, and opens any person. We cannot be afraid to ask for too much, just as Jesus did not fear he might give too much.

One way the practice of loving-kindness can be expressed is with a prayer recited each evening by the whole family. It is reminiscent to most of us already of childhood bedside prayers in which we prayed for God's blessings for each family member near and far. The extension of prayer beyond local limits is not new. Loving-kindness builds on that original traditional style and deepens it.

The practice of mindfulness is an adjunct to loving-kindness since it helps us remain present in the moment. Mindfulness meditation happens as we focus on our breathing in and out rather than entertaining our thoughts and becoming bound by the layers of ego that so ruthlessly seek to gain control of our minds. We free ourselves of distractions not by being bouncers or critics but simply by returning to an awareness of our breathing. Gradually, we exchange our ego-centered thoughts with here-and-now presence. Our practice of loving-kindness rounds out the transformation by replacing any vindictive plans with kindly ones. Whenever we think ill of someone, we amend a critical thought with a prayer that the person become enlightened and responsive to grace.

Both mindfulness and loving-kindness are originally Buddhist practices that are easily adapted to Christian devotional life. Father Bede Griffiths, OSB, reminds us that we need not be afraid to learn from other traditions: "Without Christianity I don't think oriental religions, Hinduism and Buddhism, can answer the needs of the modern world. But without the enrichment of the mystical traditions of Asia I doubt whether the Western churches can really discover the fullness of Christ which we are seeking."

Here is a fourfold Sacred Heart devotion of loving-kindness:

1. Loving-kindness in the Christian view is simply the practice of extending your prayer life to include others in anything you ask for yourself. Whenever you pray or use affirmations for yourself, extend your prayer or affirmation to include first those you love, then those with whom you have difficulty, then the whole world. For example, if you pray for the grace to face an

illness with courage and patience, you extend your prayer to include all friends, enemies, and others who might be facing the same issue: "I ask for this grace for myself, for those I love, for those to whom I am indifferent, for my enemies, and for all beings everywhere. May we all have courage and patience in the face of our illnesses. May we all handle them with equanimity and look for the graces they may have in store for us. May the heart of Jesus beat in every human breast."

2. "Pray for those who persecute you" is lived out precisely by the practice of loving-kindness. When someone acts in a hurtful or disrespectful way toward you, send him a blessing instead of a curse. For instance, if someone cuts you off in traffic, do not swear at him and aggressively lean on your horn. Instead, pray that he arrives safely and does not harm anyone. This will feel false at first because you may still be caught in road rage—that is, insulted-ego rage—but gradually it will become easier and soon you will be truly sincere in your wishing others the best. Likewise, when watching the news and seeing a national or world leader you dislike, do not say, "He is stupid" or "evil," but rather, "May he become converted to Christ's way and become a pioneer of peace." This is converting insult to prayer.

Use this same technique toward those who are kind to you or to those you respect. Show appreciation directly and verbally but then also include a prayer for their spiritual growth and happiness. End your practice by commending the person who disturbed or who has helped you to the Sacred Heart.

3. You can make a commitment to Christ to no longer engage in retaliation, even in small ways, but to return blessing for hurt. At the same time, you do not let people humiliate you or take advantage of you but you protect yourself and your personal boundaries. You might pray this way: "I protect my heart. Jesus protect my heart." When someone is mean to you, engage with him nonviolently. Then say silently: "May he find the

love in Jesus' heart and may he let go of hurting others." This may feel forced at first because you may still be caught in the wish to retaliate, but gradually it will become a feature of who you really are, Christ by grace, and you will be truly genuine in giving your blessing. You will like yourself more and, paradoxically, you will let go of your ego-centeredness more easily. End the practice by commending whoever has hurt you to the Sacred Heart of Jesus.

4. We can join the mystics in these three prayers or affirmations that foster loving-kindness:

> "I shape my heart like that of others that I meet and theirs like mine." —*St. Teresa of Avila*

> "Inflame my heart with the divine love with which your own is all on fire." —*St. Margaret Mary*

> "Jesus, I love you for the extensions of your body and soul to the farthest corners of creation through grace, through life, and through matter....I love you as a world, as this world, which has captivated my heart. And it is you, I now realize, that my fellow humans, even those who do not believe, sense and seek throughout the magic immensities of the cosmos."
> —*Teilhard de Chardin*

The Practice of Spiritual Imagination

Intuition suddenly bursts out of the piled-up facts.
—Pierre Teilhard de Chardin

Mystics have visions; so can we. Visions may take the form of discernment, intuition, and self-discovery. Every once in awhile we seem to receive messages that come from nowhere we can locate or name. They may happen in prayer or contemplation, or in the midst of ordinary mundane events. Revelations also reach us in events, people, and dreams, and in synchronicity: meaningful and unsought coincidence. These revelations usually have an image attached to them. Such revelations have a quality that is sure, grounded, nonemotional, yet clear, concise, and somehow directive. Such revelations stand out as different from normal thought processes. They are not the result of logic but come from the Higher Self, God within us. Such visions are trustworthy when they become pathways to virtue and wisdom rather than endorsements of our own pride.

St. Augustine, in his *Confessions,* shows that his memory and his imagination helped him resolve and let go of his past. This transition from attachment to the past into a new way of life was his redemption. This is also how our own active imagination can help us spiritually. The technique of active imagination can become a form of devotion since it makes images personal and we speak to them prayerfully. Jungian psychologist James Hillman writes this fascinating statement: "Contemplation of the Sacred Heart leads one beyond personal subjective feeling, expanding character toward charity, pity, and mercy." He calls the human heart the primary organ of imagination, which mediates the role of images in the life of the soul.

Imagination helps us survive in early life since our visualizing Mommy when she is not there grants us security in her absence. Later in life we find ways to imagine kindness in the midst of unkindness, loyalty in the midst of disloyalty, peace in a world of war, God in the midst of silence. This is a central achievement of sanity psychologically and of sanctity spiritually.

Active imagination opens our intuitive faculty. Here is a technique for active imagination to be done in writing with the image of the Sacred Heart of Jesus. Use it also for other images that speak to you in spiritual ways:

- Ask for the grace to let your heart become clear and open.
- Dialogue with the Sacred Heart in the image and let it speak back to you, being sure to ask what it wants you to know or do.
- Find a felt sense of the Sacred Heart within yourself and visualize yourself acting in accord with it.
- Amplify the image of the Heart of Jesus through each of your senses so that it becomes more than it ever was originally.
- Show thanks for whatever revelation or help has come to you.

Prayers

In the nineteenth century, a book was published in the Eastern Orthodox world by an anonymous monk. It recommended a five-point spiritual practice: to visualize God's presence, to use a mantra or prayer continually, to clear the mind of distractions, to focus the heart on spiritual progress, and to show universal love. The mantra or prayer is: "Lord Jesus Christ, have mercy on me a sinner." (We can substitute *seeker* for *sinner.*) The fascinating thing about this prayer is that it has been shown to activate the heart toward love. By repeating it until it matches the rhythm of our heartbeat, it induces compassion for others.

Here is a litany to recite or use for meditation. It may pull together some of what we have seen in this book so far:

Heart of Jesus, in whom there is only yes, live through me for the good of all humanity.

Heart of Jesus, from the Heart of Mary, live through me for the good of all humanity.

Heart of Jesus—center, source, and destiny of my heart—live through me for the good of all humanity.

Heart of Jesus, gate of paradise, live through me for the good of all humanity.

Heart of Jesus, aglow with divine love, live through me for the good of all humanity.

Heart of Jesus, worthy of unending honor, live through me for the good of all humanity.

Heart of Jesus, treasury of wisdom and knowledge, live through me for the good of all humanity.

Heart of Jesus, from whose fullness we all receive, live through me for the good of all humanity.

Heart of Jesus, desire of the everlasting hills, live through me for the good of all humanity.

Heart of Jesus, life-force of nature and the universe, live through me for the good of all humanity.

Heart of Jesus, patient and most merciful, live through me for the good of all humanity.

Heart of Jesus, bountiful to all who turn to you, live through me for the good of all humanity.

Heart of Jesus, fountain of grace and holiness, live through me for the good of all humanity.

Heart of Jesus, loving intent behind every twist of fate, live through me for the good of all humanity.

Heart of Jesus—pierced to open, never to close—live through me for the good of all humanity.

Heart of Jesus, source of all consolation, live through me for the good of all humanity.

Heart of Jesus—my life, my death, and my resurrection—live through me for the good of all humanity.

Heart of Jesus—pledge of tenderness, end of punishment—live through me for the good of all humanity.

Heart of Jesus, exemplar of healthy love of ourselves, live through me for the good of all humanity.

Heart of Jesus, refuge from fear and grasping, live through me for the good of all humanity.

Heart of Jesus, refuge of loving-kindness and healing, live through me for the good of all humanity.

Heart of Jesus—who embraces all and abandons none—live through me for the good of all humanity.

Heart of Jesus, abiding harmony of the universe, live through me for the good of all humanity.

Love makes God long for us....God never began to love us....We have always been...known and loved without beginning.

—Juliana of Norwich

Epilogue

FINDING GRACE AND FREEDOM FROM FEAR

I saw Him in my house. Among all the everyday things He appeared
unexpectedly and became utterly united and merged with me,
and leaped over to me without anything in between, as fire to iron,
as light to glass. And He made me like fire and like light.
And I became that which I saw before and beheld from afar.
I do not know how to relate this miracle to you.
I am man by nature, and God by grace.
—Saint Simeon the Younger

Devotion to the Sacred Heart has always included the sense
of a promise that we will find grace, protection, and guidance on
our path. St. Margaret Mary shares this stupendous revelation:

He showed me that it was his great desire to be loved
by us and to save us from the path of ruin...so he
formed the design of manifesting his heart to us, with
all the treasures of love, of mercy, of grace, of sanctification and salvation which it contains, in order that
those who desire to render him and procure for him
all the honor and love possible, might themselves be
abundantly enriched with those divine treasures of
which this heart is the source.

Knowing we are loved boosts our immune system because it gives us a sense of being accompanied rather than isolated. This aligns with a universal religious belief in the abiding presence of God. We are freed from fear by trusting a reliable and unending relationship between ourselves and God as a power higher than our ego. We can see how a personal devotion fosters this sense of trust: "They shall all sit under their own vines and under their own fig trees, and no one shall make them afraid" (Mic 4:4).

In Psalm 23, King David, addressing God as the Good Shepherd, says "I will fear no evil for you are with me." This means it is a given that we will indeed walk through dark valleys but that we do not do so alone. We are *accompanied* through the dark shadows. We are not exempted from the dark journey, but we are assured that God *joins* us in our suffering. Indeed, suffering has always been one of the ways humans have been led to religion. *When we see that God is suffering too, we realize that spirituality does not offer an end to suffering but a companion in it.*

A spiritual life does not guarantee that we will have no fear nor does it fully eliminate fear. It is not about reduction. It is about feeling the sum of all our human feelings. Then spiritual consciousness adds the dimension of accompaniment. We find ways to live *with* fear but we are no longer stopped or driven by it. We find solace in our belief in a God who journeys with us, or a shepherd or angel who guides and guards us on the path. Devotion is our way of showing gratitude.

Romans 8:26 shows that prayer is openness to the Holy Spirit praying in us: "Likewise the Spirit helps us in our weakness; for we do not know how to pray as we ought, but that very Spirit intercedes with sighs too deep for words." Our prayer can develop and advance as we trust the presence of God in our lives. "Give me what I want" becomes "Let me open myself to receive what is already and always being given to me." There is a direct connection between true prayer and grace. Once we see that all that happens is a grace, we no longer have to ask for what we need. We trust all is happening just as it needs to and our prayer is one of thanks. "Your Father knows what you need before you ask" (Matt 6:8).

In the depths of ourselves we know that the ego and its arrogance are not all there is to us. A hidden life with vast dimension and possibility is in us. The inner life of Christ in us is a mirror of and a call to our true destiny. Now we see that openness to grace is how the ego is transcended. By grace, we move out of our local citadel of *I-me-mine* to a limitless kingdom of cosmos. Like revelation, grace is intrinsic, not extrinsic; that is, not from outside forces but from deep within the spiritual Self, God within us and everywhere around us.

Grace is ever-available since God is always creating us and always sustaining us. Grace does not replace freedom but fulfills it by releasing our greatest potential. Grace divinizes human existence. Grace in our lives means that nothing is only what it appears to be but infinite in its core or heart. Grace motivates and assists us but then it is up to us to join in by our efforts and spiritual practices. Grace shows us that our destiny is not of the ego's making and shows us too that wholeness is not due to effort. All our work, both psychological and spiritual, is ultimately spiritual since we are a unity and our whole being is affected by growth in either area. In fact, theologian Karl Rahner said that grace is indistinguishable from the tendency in the human spirit to transcend ego-desire, self-absorption, or fear—our psychological work.

Grace is the light that keeps getting through. We do not have to *make* it come through, only *let* it through. I still believe, even after all the dark events of recent times, that we humans can really trust that, deep down, we are a most pure light of consciousness and bliss. We do not have to search for this light, only open ourselves to the Sacred Heart of the world and it will beam through. Then we can direct it with indefatigable compassion to our fellow pilgrims.

Something,
We know not what,
Is always and everywhere
Lovingly at work,
We know not how,
To make the world more than it is now,
To make us more than we are yet.
That Something is at once
Divine Spirit, life force of the universe,
And our own unique aliveness:
One Sacred Heart
Never apart.

Appendix I

THE APOSTLESHIP
OF PRAYER

The Apostleship of Prayer began in France, in 1844, by Francis X. Gautrelet. In 1861 Reverend Henry Ramière, SJ, made it available to parishes mainly through his book *The Apostleship of Prayer*. In 1879 the association was approved by Pius IX, and in 1896 by Leo XIII. Popes since then have continued to bless the work of the Apostleship. Its purpose is to foster the practice of prayer for the intentions of all its members and especially for the monthly intentions of the pope. Among its many practices of prayer are a daily offering of one's prayers and good works for the intentions of the Holy Father, participation in a Holy Hour, and reception of the Eucharist. The Apostleship of Prayer remains a Jesuit organization, which publishes the *Messenger of the Sacred Heart*. There are also centers called Leagues of the Sacred Heart all over the world. These publish leaflets that recommend monthly practices for the members. To become a member requires only having one's name listed in the register of a local center, which is often in a parish.

There are now over 62,500 local centers in the world; close to 7,000 are in the United States. The Association has more than 25,000,000 members, with about 4,000,000 in America. The Apostleship has been an important and immensely helpful organization since it has fostered devotion to the Sacred Heart with an accent on mutual consciousness of prayer intentions in the world community. The intentions of the pope bring an especially deep sense of social awareness to the practice. The Society of Jesus was ardently present, especially in France, at the great burgeoning of devotion to the Sacred Heart of Jesus and has remained loyal to spreading the devotion ever since. The Apostleship of Prayer is a centerpiece of that important work.

For information, visit the website: *http://www.apostles ofprayer.org.*

Appendix II

THE PIONEER TOTAL ABSTINENCE ASSOCIATION OF THE SACRED HEART

A pledge is a promise, a commitment, a vow, a consecration to an ongoing practice. The word *vow* comes from the same Latin word as *devotion: devovere.* Recall that vows have lifetime intention but they are affirmed for only one day at a time.

Here is an example of a devotion to the Sacred Heart that is based on a pledge or vow: An Irish Jesuit, James Cullen, over one hundred years ago, founded the Pioneer Total Abstinence Association of the Sacred Heart (PTAA). He chose the word *pioneer* in admiration of the American westward movement and because the words applied to Jesus: "the pioneer and perfecter of our faith" (Heb 12:2). The movement now boasts hundreds of thousands of members in Ireland and across the world. Father Cullen believed that devotion to the Sacred Heart, in the spirit of St. Ignatius, could dramatically change Irish drinking habits. He saw alcoholism as a demon that could only be exorcised by prayer and by fasting in the form of abstinence (see Mark 9:29).

Lifelong consecrated abstinence is the commitment of the members. They are supported by the prayers and spiritual support of all who practice devotion to the Sacred Heart. Father

Cullen tapped into the style of self-sacrifice and reparation that characterized the devotion of his time. His prayer of offering, recited twice daily, says: "For your greater glory and consolation, O Sacred Heart of Jesus, for your sake to give good example, to practice self-denial, to make reparation to you for the sins of intemperance and for the conversion of excessive drinkers, I will abstain for life from all intoxicating drinks. Amen."

Members pledge total abstinence for life from all alcoholic drinks; as a visible sign of their commitment they wear an emblem or badge of the Sacred Heart. The Pioneers are a community program because they include not only alcoholics but family and friends who want to help them by joining in. Some do this by taking the pledge themselves and others by honoring the badge and not forcing a drink on a Pioneer.

When Alcoholics Anonymous arrived in Ireland in 1946, director of the Pioneers Father Daniel Dargan SJ, saw the two movements as complementary of one another. Both AA and PTAA have benefited Irish life and increased consciousness of the need for a spiritual program as the only reliable way to deal with alcohol and, more recently, drugs. Vast numbers of people over the years have promised to abstain from alcohol in honor of the Sacred Heart. In Ireland today 8 percent of the population are Pioneers and a further 17 percent abstain for other reasons.

Ask yourself whether this program fits you. If so, you can find out more online or locally. Ask yourself about the possibility of other vows that may be important to your spiritual growth. For instance, you may want to make a vow of nonviolence or nonretaliation in all your dealings with others. You may want to vow spreading devotion to the Sacred Heart. You may want to vow lifelong examination of the scripture in study groups. You may want to vow to set aside a period of your life to enter the service of others in a public program or as a missionary helper.

In any case, it is necessary to pray and meditate on your plan for at least a month before making your vow. When you do make the vow, it is important to do it in response to a call of grace, within a ritual setting, with family or fellow faith witnesses, and with a solemn and joyous celebration that is planned beforehand. Begin with a one-year vow, if that seems more reasonable and appropriate to you. A vow is not to be construed as self-coercion. It is a liberating commitment. You can tell it is real when it brings an abiding and serene joy as well as certitude that you are finally doing what you have been called to for a long time. A vow or pledge states aloud what you truly have become by grace.

"As we felt new power flow in, as we enjoyed peace of mind, as we discovered we could face life successfully, as we became conscious of His presence, we began to lose our fear of today, tomorrow, or the hereafter. We were reborn."
—Alcoholics Anonymous

Appendix III

THE LITANY OF THE SACRED HEART OF JESUS

Reciting the Litany of the Sacred Heart is a form of devotion that includes repetition. We can choose the aspiration that fits our life situation here and now and keep reciting it throughout the day as a mantra. The aspirations in the traditional litany summarize the love of God for us in the history of salvation. An alternative litany may be found at the end of chapter 5. It is also useful to form one's own litany of the Sacred Heart of Jesus based on one's own meditations.

Meditating on the titles of Jesus in the litany deepens our devotion to the Sacred Heart; each title is found in scripture:

Heart of Jesus, Son of the Eternal Father:

"And a voice came from heaven, 'You are my Son, the Beloved; with you I am well pleased'" (Mark 1:11).

Heart of Jesus, formed by the Holy Spirit in the womb of the Virgin Mother:

"The angel said to her, 'The Holy Spirit will come upon you, and the power of the Most High will overshadow you; therefore the child to be born will be holy; he will be called Son of God'" (Luke 1:35).

Heart of Jesus, substantially united to the Word of God:
"In the beginning was the Word, and the Word was with God, and the Word was God" (John 1:1).

Heart of Jesus, sacred temple of God:
"Jesus answered them, 'Destroy this temple, and in three days I will raise it up'" (John 2:19).

Heart of Jesus, tabernacle of the Most High:
"And the Word became flesh and lived among us, and we have seen his glory, the glory as of a father's only son, full of grace and truth" (John 1:14).

Heart of Jesus, house of God and gate of heaven:
"And he [Jacob] was afraid, and said, 'How awesome is this place! This is none other than the house of God, and this is the gate of heaven'" (Genesis 28:17).

Heart of Jesus, glowing furnace of charity:
"The crucible is for silver, and the furnace is for gold, so a person is tested by being praised [for showing goodness]" (Proverbs 27:21).

Heart of Jesus, abode of justice and love:
"Hope does not disappoint us, because God's love has been poured into our hearts through the Holy Spirit that has been given to us" (Romans 5:5).

Heart of Jesus, full of goodness and love:
"I give you a new commandment, that you love one another. Just as I have loved you, you also should love one another" (John 13:34).

Heart of Jesus, abyss of all virtues:
"And all in the crowd were trying to touch him, for power [virtue] came out from him and healed all of them" (Luke 6:19).

Heart of Jesus, most worthy of all praise:

"They sing a new song: 'You are worthy to take the scroll and to open its seals, for you were slaughtered and by your blood you ransomed for God saints from every tribe and language and people and nation'" (Rev 5:9).

Heart of Jesus, in whom are all the treasures of wisdom and knowledge:

"I want their hearts to be encouraged and united in love, so that they may have all the riches of assured understanding and have the knowledge of God's mystery, that is, Christ himself, in whom are hidden all the treasures of wisdom and knowledge" (Col 2:2–3).

Heart of Jesus, in whom the Father was well pleased

"And a voice from heaven said, 'This is my Son, the Beloved, with whom I am well pleased'" (Matt 3:17).

Heart of Jesus, of whose fullness we have all received:

"From his fullness we have all received, grace upon grace" (John 1:16).

Heart of Jesus, desire of the everlasting hills:

"The blessings of your father are stronger than the blessings of the eternal mountains, the bounties of the everlasting hills; may they be on the head of Joseph, on the brow of him who was set apart from his brothers" (Gen 49:26).

Heart of Jesus, patient and most merciful:

"Rend your hearts and not your clothing. Return to the Lord, your God, for he is gracious and merciful, slow to anger, and abounding in steadfast love, and relents from punishing" (Joel 2:13).

Heart of Jesus, enriching all who invoke you:
"For there is no distinction between Jew and Greek; the same Lord is Lord of all and is generous to all who call on him" (Rom 10:12).

Heart of Jesus, fountain of life and holiness:
"With joy you will draw water from the wells of salvation" (Isa 12:3).

Heart of Jesus, propitiation for our sins:
"My little children, I am writing these things to you so that you may not sin. But if anyone does sin, we have an advocate with the Father, Jesus Christ the righteous; and he is the atoning sacrifice for our sins, and not for ours only but also for the sins of the whole world" (1 John 1–2).

Heart of Jesus, loaded down with opprobrium:
"To give one's cheek to the smiter, and be filled with insults" (Lam 3:30).

Heart of Jesus, bruised for our offenses:
"But he was wounded for our transgressions, crushed for our iniquities; upon him was the punishment that made us whole, and by his bruises we are healed" (Isa 53:5).

Heart of Jesus, obedient to death:
"He humbled himself and became obedient to the point of death—even death on a cross" (Phil 2:8).

Heart of Jesus, pierced with a lance:
"Instead, one of the soldiers pierced his side with a spear, and at once blood and water came out" (John 19:34).

Heart of Jesus, source of all consolation:
"Blessed be the God and Father of our Lord Jesus Christ, the Father of mercies and the God of all consolation" (2 Cor 1:3).

Heart of Jesus, our life and resurrection:
"Jesus said to her [Martha], 'I am the resurrection and the life. Those who believe in me, even though they die, will live'" (John 11:25).

Heart of Jesus, our peace and reconciliation:
"For in him all the fullness of God was pleased to dwell, and through him God was pleased to reconcile to himself all things, whether on earth or in heaven, by making peace through the blood of his cross" (Col 1:19–20).

Heart of Jesus, victim for our sins:
"This is my blood of the covenant, which is poured out for many for the forgiveness of sins" (Matt 26:28).

Heart of Jesus, salvation of those who trust in you,
"You have heard of this hope before in the word of the truth, the gospel" (Col 1:5).

Heart of Jesus, hope of those who die in you:
"To them God chose to make known how great among the Gentiles are the riches of the glory of this mystery, which is Christ in you, the hope of glory" (Col 1:27).

Heart of Jesus, delight of all the saints:
"I was beside him, like a master worker; and I was daily his delight, rejoicing before him always" (Prov 8:30).

SELECTED BIBLIOGRAPHY

Au, Wilkie, and Noreen Cannon Au. *The Discerning Heart: Exploring the Christian Path*. Mahwah, NJ: Paulist Press, 2006.

Bainvel, J. V., SJ. *Devotion to the Sacred Heart of Jesus: The Doctrine and Its History*. London: Burns & Oates Ltd., 1924.

Broderick, Robert, ed. *The Catholic Encyclopedia*. Nashville: T. Nelson Reference, 1990.

Campbell, Karen J., ed. *German Mystical Writings*. New York: Continuum, 1991.

Chevalier, Jean, and John Gheerbrant. *Dictionary of Symbols*. New York: Penguin, 1996.

Cross, F., and E. A. Livingstone. *The Oxford Dictionary of the Christian Church*. New York: Oxford University Press, 2005.

Edinger, Edward. *The Christian Archetype*. Toronto: Inner City Books, 1987.

Griffiths, Bede. *Essential Writings*. Maryknoll, NY: Orbis Books, 2004.

James, William. *The Varieties of Religious Experience*. London: Longmans, Green & Co, 1902. Reprint New York: Simon and Schuster, 1997.

Keating, Thomas. *The Mystery of Christ: The Liturgy as a Religious Experience*. Rockport, MA: Element, 1987.

King, Thomas M. *Teilhard's Mass: Approaches to "The Mass on the World."* New York / Mahwah, NJ: Paulist Press, 2005.

Rahner, Karl. *Foundations of Christian Faith*. New York: Herder and Herder, 1982.

Rahner, Karl, and Philip Endean. *Spiritual Writings*. Maryknoll, NY: Orbis Books, 2004.

Schillebeeckx, Edward. *Church: The Human Story of God*. New York: Crossroad, 1991.

Smith, Huston. *The World's Religions*. San Francisco: Harper, 1991.

Stepaniants, Marietta T., and Seyyed Hossein Nasr, eds. *Sufi Wisdom*. New York: State University of New York Press, 1994.

Teasdale, Wayne, and Beatrice Bruteau, eds. *The Mystic Heart: Discovering a Universal Spirituality in the World's Religions*. Novato, CA: New World Library, 2001.

Teilhard de Chardin, Pierre. *The Divine Milieu*. 1960. Reprint New York: Harper Perennial, 2001.

————. *The Future of Man*. 1964. Reprint New York: Doubleday/Image, 2004.

————. *The Phenomenon of Man*. 1964. Reprint New York: Harper Perennial, 1976.

————. *Toward the Future*. San Diego: Harcourt/Harvest, 2002.

Wilber, Ken. *The Marriage of Sense and Soul: Integrating Science and Religion*. New York: Random House, 1998.

Williams, Margaret, RSCJ. *The Sacred Heart in the Life of the Church*. New York: Sheed & Ward, 1957.

David Richo, PhD, was ordained a priest in 1966 and now works as a psychotherapist and workshop leader in Santa Barbara and San Francisco, California.

He is the author of—

How to Be an Adult: A Handbook for Psychological and Spiritual Integration (Paulist Press, 1991)

When Love Meets Fear: Becoming Defense-less and Resource-full (Paulist Press, 1997)

Shadow Dance: Liberating the Power and Creativity of Your Dark Side (Shambhala, 1999)

Catholic Means Universal: Integrating Spirituality and Religion (Crossroad, 2000)

Mary Within: A Jungian Contemplation of Her Titles and Powers (Crossroad, 2001)

How to Be an Adult in Relationships (Shambhala, 2002)

The Five Things We Cannot Change and the Happiness We Find by Embracing Them (Shambhala, 2005)

The Power of Coincidence: How Life Shows Us What We Need (Shambhala, 2007)

For a catalog of tapes and CDs of live classes, visit

davericho.com